PRAISE FO

Conspiracy of Kindness

Conspiracy of Kindness explains one of the absolute best biblical methods of reaching out to the unconnected without any trace of bigotry or superiority.

BILL EASUM
President, Easum, Bandy & Associates (www.easumbandy.com)

This classic book leads us into non-threatening love actions that release the power of the gospel to transform lives forever.

DALE GALLOWAY
Dean, The Beeson International Center
Asbury Theological Seminary

Steve Sjogren makes it both practical and enjoyable simply to be kind. What a refreshing approach to expressing the love of God to everyday people.

DUDLEY HALL
Author and President of the Fellowship of Connected Churches
and Ministries

Steve Sjogren's *Conspiracy of Kindness* has made a great contribution to churches everywhere that wanted to reach out but needed new ways to do it and new ways to involve people who had never reached out before. The fact that servant evangelism was modeled through his Cincinnati Vineyard church grounds the book in reality, and the book's many examples give us viable options. This book has awakened the entrepreneurial spirit in some churches, who then invented outreach ministries that Steve never thought of! This new edition assures the book's continued influence.

GEORGE HUNTER
School of World Mission and Evangelism
Asbury Theological Seminary

In *Conspiracy of Kindness*, the genius of Steve Sjogren shines. He gives readers an uncomplicated, fun way to get the whole church doing evangelism. Steve shows us how to lower the "E-word" hurdle so that even those who don't have the gift of evangelism can participate. I'm telling you, it's genius . . .

TODD HUNTER
National Director, Alpha USA

Most Christians become paralyzed just thinking about evangelism. But relax! Steve Sjogren will show you how to demonstrate God's love in practical ways. It's so easy, you will be motivated and equipped to join with other believers in the conspiracy of kindness.

ROBERT E. LOGAN
Founder, CoachNet
Coauthor, *Releasing Your Church's Potential*

There are two things I especially love about servant evangelism: first, what it does for those who are served, showing them a kind face of Christianity (as opposed to an angry or argumentative face), and second, what it does for those who serve. It builds in them an identity as servants, which I think must make Jesus smile. May the conspiracy of kindness spread!

BRIAN MCLAREN
Author, *Everything Must Change*
www.brianmclaren.net

Do you like the idea of reaching people for Christ, but fear the process? In this straightforward and powerful book, Steve Sjogren presents practical ideas every one of us can use. The results can be dramatic— and have an impact for all of eternity. So read the book, join the conspiracy, roll up your sleeves, and watch God work!

MARK MITTELBERG
Author, *Building a Contagious Church*
Former Evangelism Leader, Willow Creek Association

For years, *Conspiracy of Kindness* has been spiritual leaven in the Church. *Conspiracy of Kindness* has worked its way into the heart and life of the American Church, stimulating the release of God's grace and love. *Conspiracy of Kindness* is more than theory. "Conspiracy" means "to breathe with," and Steve Sjogren's book has indeed started a conspiracy by assisting the Church to partner with the Spirit to breathe out the love of God into a world that desperately needs to know God's love.

BERT WAGGONER
National Director, Vineyard USA
Senior Pastor, Vineyard Church, Sugar Land, Texas

Conspiracy of
Kindness

A Unique Approach to

SHARING

the Love of Jesus

Steve Sjogren

Regal

From Gospel Light
Ventura, California, U.S.A.

Published by Regal
From Gospel Light
Ventura, California, U.S.A.
www.regalbooks.com
Printed in the U.S.A.

First edition published by Servant Publications in 1993.
Second edition published by Regal Books in 2003.
Third edition published by Regal Books in 2007.

Library of Congress Cataloging-in-Publication Data
The Library of Congress has catalogued the second edition as follows:
Sjogren, Steve, 1955-
 Conspiracy of kindness: a refreshing new approach to sharing the love of Jesus / Steve Sjogren.
   p. cm.
 Originally published: Ann Arbor, Mich.: Vine Books, c2003.
 ISBN 978-08307-4572-2
 1. Evangelistic work. 2. Kindness—Religious aspects—Christianity. I. Title
 BV3793.S486 2004
 269'.2—dc22
                                                          2004000701

Rights for publishing this book outside the U.S.A. or in non-English languages are administered by Gospel Light Worldwide, an international not-for-profit ministry. For additional information, please visit www.glww.org, email info@glww.org, or write to Gospel Light Worldwide, 1957 Eastman Avenue, Ventura, CA 93003, U.S.A.

To Janie, my wife—you are lovely and talented. Thanks for showing me the patience and grace of God along the way.

To Glenna, my mom—thanks for having and sharing one of the largest hearts on the planet.

You are the two people God has used to mold my heart to the point that I have begun to notice what God is doing with people.

Contents

Acknowledgments

The concepts presented in this book come from the combined influences of many friends. Their lives have rubbed off on me. Brent Rue had the idea of the first free car wash and embodied the values of servant evangelism. John Wimber mentored me, and he expressed better than anyone what I believe about practical Christianity. Although both are now gone, I continue to be challenged by their wonderful lives. Thank you, Ken Gulliksen, for giving me a chance in the ministry and for living in the power of the conspiracy of kindness. I'm grateful for the motivational and editorial help I received from Teresa Cleary, Lynda Sims, Chris Barker, Dave Workman and Ken Wilson. Thanks, guys, for keeping me on track! Tom Philippi (Mr. Graphics-o-rama), you were always ready in season and out of season with your ideas.

Preface to the Updated Edition

Much has happened since the time *Conspiracy of Kindness* was first published. With the Internet, increasing globalization and iPods everywhere, the world is not the same place. Through it all, in recent years, the conspiracy about kindness has grown, and more people want to be kinder than ever. More individuals and churches have embraced servant evangelism, too—more than I could have ever imagined.

As the movement has grown, those of us who practice servant evangelism have learned a lot—thus the updated and expanded version of this book. Kindness is an ongoing message, not something static that is once learned, forever understood. Not something that was cool once upon a time, and then we move on. Not a program, nor a fad; rather, kindness is a lifestyle.

We see abundant evidence that where servant evangelism has been embraced, people and communities have been changed. This works with small groups and large ones, in the United States and in Cambodia, in formal settings and in everyday life. In fact, as the world village grows increasingly smaller and the commonalities of people everywhere arise, kindness is a perfect fit. Showing first, talking second—the way Jesus lived His life— seems to be more appropriate than ever.

With that, rather than talking anymore, let's proceed to showing how you can be a part of the conspiracy of kindness.

An Introduction to Kindness

Kindness is a language which the dumb can speak,
the deaf can understand.
C. N. BOVEE

Christians in America have long been preoccupied with possible conspiracies against the Church. Since coming to Christ in 1974, I have heard of at least 10 such plots, theories that reflect various levels of creativity and credibility. One widespread rumor was started by an evangelist who claimed to be a former member of the Illuminati, a satanic cult bent on infiltrating the Church. This man became discredited overnight when his story was proved to be influenced by LSD.

Another Christian conspiracy revolved around Madalyn Murray O'Hair, a vocal proponent of atheism. O'Hair supposedly had launched a secret campaign with the Federal Communications Commission to get Christian broadcasting off the air. A couple of times each year, someone would approach me for permission to circulate a petition to stop this action. When I called the FCC to investigate, I discovered something interesting: To their knowledge no such campaign has *ever* existed, yet they have been receiving petitions from zealous Christians for the past 30-some years!

The conspiracy theory I've heard about most often concerns the logo of Procter and Gamble, Cincinnati's largest and oldest company. The image depicts a crescent moon and several stars. Coined in the 1800s, it represents the 13 original colonies, yet many Christians over the years have claimed that this company logo stands for the occult. No matter how often Procter and Gamble expresses its true intention, the rumors continue. Some fear-mongers claim that any naive persons who would dare use Crest toothpaste are thereby supporting the New Age movement and exposing themselves to possible demon possession! The truth is, the only thing anyone will get from using Crest is clean teeth.

A GODLY CONSPIRACY

I believe there have been few authentic conspiracies against the Church, yet we can all bet the family farm that such stories will continue to thrive. But my point in this book isn't to stand on top of a soapbox. In fact, one conspiracy really *is* going on today, but not one most of us can readily see. It has gone on quietly, almost unnoticed, at work in the hearts of millions of people without their knowledge. This movement dates back almost 2,000 years, drawing unwitting outsiders toward a faith they haven't consciously embraced. Furthermore, agents of this conspiracy can be found just about everywhere. They are among us, possibly sitting right beside us in church pews. Even some pastors are involved in this secret movement.

Before you type up a petition, I should tell you that this conspiracy is a godly one. Paul spoke of it in his letter to the Romans: "God's kindness is meant to lead you to repentance" (Rom. 2:4, *RSV*). This book is all about that conspiracy—*a conspiracy of kindness.*

God is seeking to enter the heart of every person on this planet, but He faces a significant obstacle to His conspiracy. The problem has never been the message; we have that straight, for the most part. Nor is God's problem the lack of an audience; plenty of people need to hear good news. His problem is the reluctant army He calls the Church. God is looking for people who are willing to participate in acts of love and kindness to those outside of their present circle. He is looking for people who believe that a humble demonstration of love plants a seed of eternity in the hearts of others that will blossom into faith in Christ.

The strategy of this conspiracy operates on the premise that God is passionately in love with unbelievers. As dynamic seeds of kindness are planted in their hearts, the Holy Spirit will pursue them. We are the sowers of those seeds of love. God is the farmer who oversees the entire process.

I certainly do not intend to criticize anyone who is sharing the gospel in other ways. I believe that all honest approaches to evangelism work if people just keep at them. I encourage you to share the gospel *more* with your world, using whatever approach works for you. Clearly, the state of evangelism today doesn't demand a *few* good ideas but a *hundred*.

This book compiles the observations and lessons that my congregation and I learned over the years as we sought to share the good news throughout the city of Cincinnati. I believe that you will be encouraged by the story of what has happened there. Many of these ideas will be new to you. I hope that you can see past the newness and resist the temptation to reject whatever may differ from your established ways of viewing evangelism.

A New Vision

What approach will capture the attention of the non-Christian society around us? I believe that the message of the gospel must be *spoken* and *shown* to the watching world. Surveys and studies indicate that approximately 10 percent of Christians are naturally gifted in the ministry of evangelism. In this book, I hope to present a way of reaching the unchurched that can be done easily by the other 90 percent.

In our search for greater effectiveness, we cannot retreat from sharing the message of the gospel. The only negotiable point is what *approach* we should take. Lowering the entrance requirements to faith in Jesus in order to make the gospel message more palatable will ultimately backfire on the Church and rob the gospel of its power. We don't want to tamper with the *what* of the gospel message, but we do need to examine the *how*.

A great message doesn't count for much unless we have an audience that is listening. Christian researcher George Barna once wrote a powerful booklet titled *We Have Seen the Future: The Demise of Christianity in Los Angeles County*.[1] In this book, Barna stated that in spite of the appearance of large and very visible churches, the local church has gradually ceased to influence the secular community around it. Barna warned that if change didn't occur soon, the Church in Los Angeles would emit zero influence on the surrounding world—a pattern that could be repeated across the nation.

My goal is to present a new vision and a simple strategy for sharing the message of Jesus' love in a way that will change people's lives forever. My aim is to stir up in you a heart to obey God by sharing the good news with those around you. I pray that these ideas will fuel your courage to step out of your safety zone and begin to meet the needs of a desperate and hurting world.

THE BIG ADVENTURE CONTINUES

While pastoring the Vineyard Community Church in Cincinnati, I began to explore evangelism in a way that was new to me. After helping to start churches in two previous cities, my wife, Janie, and I thought we had a handle on how to do it. I spent my first two years in Cincinnati driving a school bus and sharing my desire to launch a new church. After telling more than 1,000 people about the kind of church we envisioned, we held our first Sunday celebration. A grand total of 37 people attended—a rejection rate of about 97 percent!

By the time we celebrated our seventeenth anniversary as a Sunday morning church, we had more than 6,000 people attending five weekend celebrations. We launched 15 other churches in the Cincinnati-Dayton area—churches that touched well over 500,000 people with the love of God in a tangible way.

When we began to reap the harvest of seeds sown with acts of kindness, our church began to grow. It wasn't long before every day seemed a little like the opening scenes of *Indiana Jones and the Raiders of the Lost Ark*. In this metaphor, I am Indiana (not too big a stretch for you, right?). Every day was filled with snakes, huge boulders rolling toward me and tribes of armed natives chasing me—and that was just the church staff! If that seems negative, let me assure you that everything that was happening at the time far outweighed the risk of what comes with growth. Besides, we were just listening and following the inspired thoughts given to us by God.

And so, a couple of decades or so later, we are still in a Jesus adventure. Our latest installment is the Kindness.com initiative, sponsored by ConspiracyofKindness.com. (If you have an Internet connection, you can go to www.conspiracyofkindness.com/adventure to hear a special message from me to you.)

Here's the idea: Why not enlist hundreds—or maybe even thousands—of Christ-followers in a grass-roots ad-hoc initiative to reach not-yet believers directly? This means that regardless of whether or not your church has a formal servant evangelism "program," you can personally join the Conspiracy of Kindness, right now, today, with the simple click of a mouse and the entry of some rudimentary information.

"Well," you say, "what will I need to do?" Partners in the Kindness.com initiative agree to ask the Holy Spirit to help them notice people they encounter every day and to begin to show those people acts of kindness as a practical demonstration of God's love. Sound familiar? At the end of the book, I have included five ways that you can do this simply and naturally in your everyday life. With each act of kindness, you will deliver a connect card pointing the recipient to Kindness.com. (If you go to ConspiracyofKindness.com and give us your information, we will send you a ConspiracyofKindness.com partner's kit to get you started.)

Not-yet believers who visit Kindness.com will see a series of videos that will lead them to a starting point for a spiritual life following Christ. To those who make the request, we will send materials to help them start and keep going in their faith journey.

So don't hesitate—go to ConspiracyofKindness.com and become a co-conspirator as we recklessly fling seeds of kindness together!

Note
1. George Barna, *We Have Seen the Future: The Demise of Christianity in Los Angeles County* (Glendale, CA: Barna Research Group, 1990).

CHAPTER 1

Who Answers God's Mail?

Kind words can be short and easy to speak,
but their echoes are truly endless.
MOTHER TERESA

Keep on sowing your seed, for you never know
which will grow—perhaps it all will.
ECCLESIASTES 11:6, *TLB*

On a typical hot, humid, summer day in Cincinnati, Joe Delaney and his eight-year-old son were in the backyard playing catch. As the two lobbed the ball back and forth, Joe could tell something was on Jared's mind. At first they talked about Reds baseball, friends, and summer vacation. Then the conversation took a more serious turn, and Joe felt like a backyard ballplayer who suddenly found himself in the major leagues.

"Dad, is there a God?"

Joe had the same helpless feeling he experienced on the high school baseball team when he lost sight of a fly ball in the blazing sun. He didn't know whether to move forward, backward, or just stay put. A string of trite answers raced through his mind. In the end Joe opted for honesty. "I don't know, Jared," he replied, as the ball landed solidly in his glove.

Joe's agnosticism failed to stifle his son's curiosity. Jared dug a little deeper. "If there is a God, how would you know him?"

"I really have no idea, Jared. I only went to church a couple of times when I was a kid, so I don't know a lot about these kinds of things."

Jared seemed deep in thought for a few minutes as the game of catch continued. Suddenly, he headed for the house. "I'll be right back," he yelled over his shoulder. "I have to get something." Jared soon returned with a Mylar helium balloon fresh from the circus along with a pen and an index card.

"Jared, what in the world are you doing?" Joe asked.

"I'm going to send a message to God—airmail," the boy earnestly replied.

Before Joe could protest, his son had started writing. "Dear God," Jared wrote on the index card, "if you are real and if you are there, send people who know you to Dad and me."

Joe kept his mouth shut, not wanting to dampen his son's enthusiasm. *This is silly*, he thought as he helped Jared fasten the card to the balloon's string. *But, God, I hope You're watching*, he added to his silent petition. After Jared let go of the balloon, father and son stood with their faces to the sky and watched it sail away.

Two days later I became part of the answer to this unusual inquiry. Joe and Jared pulled into the free car wash that our church was holding as part of our outreach into the community on this particular Saturday morning. "How much?" Joe asked as he neared the line of buckets, sponges and hoses.

"It's free," I told him. "No strings attached."

"Really!" Joe exclaimed. He seemed intrigued with the idea of getting something for nothing. "But why are you doing this?"

"We just want to show you God's love in a practical way."

It was as if that simple statement opened a hidden door to Joe's heart. The look on his face was incredible. "Wait a minute!" he practically shouted. "Are you guys Christians?"

"Yeah, we're Christians," I replied.

"Are you the kind of Christians who believe in God?"

I couldn't help but smile. "Yes, we're *that* kind of Christians."

After directing a big grin at Jared, Joe proceeded to tell me the story of releasing the helium balloon with its message only days earlier. "I guess you're the answer to one of the strangest prayers God's ever received," Joe said.

"Dear God, if you are real and if you are there, send people who know you to Dad and me."

THE POWER OF KINDNESS

Joe and Jared's story is one of the thousands of examples of how servant evangelism works as a conspiracy of kindness. After many years of demonstrating these practical expressions of God's love to total strangers, it's still a thrill to see their eyes light up when they realize that our deeds of kindness are actually free, with no strings attached. As we serve people in practical ways, their attitudes toward God are affected before they even realize it. During this time I've seen hundreds of individuals like Joe open their hearts to God.

People often ask me to explain servant evangelism in a nutshell. I'm not very good at putting anything in a nutshell, but this is the definition we used in our church: *demonstrating the kindness of God by offering to do some act of humble service with no strings attached.* Let's tear that definition apart, one piece at a time.

Demonstrating the Kindness of God

Whenever people see the love of God in action, a hot button is touched deep inside them. I'm convinced they *feel* God's presence and *see* that He's real, even though they usually don't know how to respond. Some people seem to even hear something audible from the Lord when we serve them.

Jesus said, "By this all will know that you are my disciples, if you have love for one another" (John 13:35). This verse is often interpreted as a call to unity in the Body of Christ. God certainly wants us to love other believers, but Jesus' call goes far beyond those narrow boundaries. He called the disciples to love one another because the world instinctively recognizes us as followers of Jesus when we demonstrate that love for all to see.

By Offering to Do

The mere offer to serve others holds great power. For example, one of our teams was going from store to store in a large mall in Cincinnati offering to clean their restrooms. Whenever we explained what we were doing, the atmosphere around us would get quiet, like the commercial some years ago, "When E. F. Hutton speaks, everybody listens." I admit that it does look rather odd to see a couple of people come up with bucket in hand and make this offer.

One particular Saturday morning, a female shopper couldn't help but eavesdrop when our team asked permission to clean a store's toilet. She later discovered that one of the engineers at her company attends our fellowship and asked him, "What kind of Christians are you who clean toilets to show God's love? This sort of Christianity sparks my interest!"

Often, the results of our projects extended far beyond those we directly touched. When we gave away soft drinks, not everyone wanted a can. Sometimes, just one person in a group of four at a football game would receive a drink, but as they walked away the entire group would read the card and retell the story with an inquisitive look on their faces. During some of our outreach projects, we may have touched about 1,000 people, but the actual number who heard about what we did was much larger, possibly by a factor of two or three. Because the offer of service was so intriguing to people, they tended to tell their friends.

Some Act of Humble Service

Jesus came as the suffering, humble servant. The goal in servant evangelism is to shine the spotlight on God's kingdom by coming in the spirit of Jesus. God understood that humility is one of the traits that get the attention of the human race. As we give away deeds of humility, we bring a similar influence into the world. In recent years we have been operating under a new assumption: *It is normal for Christians to serve those outside the church.* As we allow Jesus to love others through us, we will find great joy in serving.

Humility seems to make sense to everyone except veteran churchgoers. Jesus' lowly state threw a curve ball to the religious leaders of His day. They expected Him to appear as victorious Lord of lords and King of kings. Of course, Jesus is coming the second time in manifest power and authority, but He came the first time in humility. Today, it seems little has changed. While we look high and low for effective approaches that will touch the world around us with God's love, the most obvious one is often overlooked. Doing humble acts of service causes the world to notice our lives and to listen to our message.

With No Strings Attached

Our service to the community was always free. Many people offered to donate to our "cause," but we always refused any repayment. To receive money for what we did would have lessened the impact of our services. Free service offered a picture of the grace of God, a priceless gift that can never be repaid.

One fall, a small group went out on several Saturday mornings raking leaves. One lady was overjoyed at our offer and said,

"You've just saved me a *big* job." With six to eight people, it doesn't take long to knock off a small yard, but that same job would have taken her hours to do alone.

When we began to leave, she wrote out a check for our services. We had said earlier that we were doing this for free, but our words hadn't registered with her. We continued to load our rakes and bags into the back of a pickup truck and she was still trying to stick her check in our pockets. It was quite a sight—right out of a Laurel and Hardy episode! Even as we were driving away, this woman was still waving her arms with her check in hand.

Free service offers a picture of the grace of God,
a priceless gift that can never be repaid.

About a week later she got the better of us by sending a check in the mail with a short note: "I told you I wanted to pay for your raking my lawn! Please use this for whatever." We kept the letter and gave the money to our ministry to the needy.

HOW DOES SERVANT EVANGELISM WORK?

I once witnessed the effectiveness of servant evangelism at an evangelism conference held in Houston. I was one of several speakers offering different ideas for spreading the good news. My part was to teach on how to step out in simple expressions of God's love to outsiders. A friend of mine, a pastor who is gifted in speaking to strangers about Christ, spoke about sharing the gospel through friendship, prayer for the sick, and open-air preaching—whatever seemed to fit each person. After talking about evangelism for a couple of days, we spent the last day actually going out to do it.

For the faint of heart, we did a free car wash, free windshield washing and a food-giveaway to single mothers. For the more courageous, we offered more traditional approaches: going door to door, taking surveys and preaching at a local park frequented by joggers. Unfortunately, the joggers paid no attention to what was being said. Not long after the preaching team began, the Houston police showed up to make sure this group had a permit to hold a meeting. Since they didn't, the police asked them to disperse. The group was disappointed, though some later admitted they were a little relieved. "At least now I don't have to talk to strangers," they reasoned.

As they started to leave, one lady announced that she had an idea, hopped into her car and drove off. Ten minutes later, she pulled up with 20 dozen Popsicles! She explained, "I just thought that there was probably no law against giving out Popsicles without a permit." The group discovered that joggers who aren't necessarily interested in listening to a stranger preach at them are completely open to talking to a stranger who offers free refreshments.

Within 20 minutes all of the Popsicles were gone. Some joggers took the Popsicles and went their way without much conversation. Others were curious: "Why are you being so nice to me? I don't even know you." "What kind of Christians are you guys anyway?"

These were not difficult questions to answer. In fact, the former preachers were thrilled to have people asking any questions at all. One man took a Popsicle and asked the "why" question with a stunned look on his face. When he was told this was to show God's love in a practical way, he began to tell his life's story to the Christian he had just met.

The case of the preachers turned Popsicle-distributors illustrates something I've seen time and again: Servant evangelism works. People on the receiving end of these simple acts of kindness come away with a more positive impression of Christianity than they previously had. With regular frequency, these deeds also open a door to deeper communication about the gospel. And those who engage in this approach to sharing God's love with strangers don't come away feeling like they've been put through a meat grinder.

Servant evangelism is one method—not the only method, nor necessarily the best one for every situation. And like any other approach, it simply doesn't work apart from the agency of the Holy Spirit who is the only true evangelist. Its effectiveness may vary from one cultural setting to another and there may well come a time when it has outlived its usefulness.

Nevertheless, in a society where other forms of sharing the gospel often meet a great deal of resistance—one that feels it's heard too much "God talk" and not seen enough "God activity"—servant evangelism seems to be a fruitful way for Christians to share God's love with their community. Our experience in Cincinnati showed us that evangelism must contain the right words, but that those words must *follow* the demonstration of the love of God. The following equation states how this approach works:

Servant evangelism =
deeds of love + words of love + adequate time

Following this sequence of *deeds* of love before *words* of love practically communicates that the experience of God's love precedes the understanding of that love. The scriptural record of His activity among the human race reflects this pattern. God does something wonderful with people, and only later—sometimes years later—do they understand or make sense of what He did. The apostles experienced the works of Jesus for three years and then spent decades making sense out of those works. As recorded in Acts 2, the Early Church experienced the coming of the Holy Spirit in power, but these same men wrote and applied this event for decades.

- *Deeds of love.* God's love must be communicated from person to person, not just from page to person. If His love could be sent through printed information alone, we could simply flood our cities with gospel tracts and then rest assured that we have done our part. Deeds of love allow us to sneak into the hearts of those we serve. Even though people aren't conscious of what's happening, they are welcoming us and the God we represent into the fortress of their hearts. Deeds of love aren't enough on their own to bring someone to Christ, but they do create "phone wires" for transmitting the spoken message.

- *Words of love.* Deeds of kindness get people's attention and often cause them to ask us questions. Instead of having a forced presentation of the gospel to people who really aren't interested in what we have to say, we find people are curious and ask us to explain what we're about after we've served them. Then we can present the message that is vital in bringing someone to Christ without taking a sales approach. When we do speak, we must be sensitive to the level of receptivity of each person and explain the words of God's love in whatever way the hearer can understand. These words are the cognitive or conscious element of our evangelism. If we don't follow our actions with words, they will only know that we are nice people, not that God loves them.

• *Adequate time.* We need to allow time for deeds and words of love to have their effect on the hearts of people. If we are allowing the Holy Spirit to do His work in His way and in His timing, we must not demand instantaneous results. We can be assured that God will not allow any seed He has sown to come back without bearing fruit (see Isa. 55:11), but He typically works over a prolonged period of time to bring sinners to Himself. As we allow adequate time for seeds of love to take root, we put the expectation for results on the right spot: the Holy Spirit.

We might ask, "How long does it take for someone to come to Christ?" The only right answer to that question is, "It takes a unique amount of time for each person." One day while attending Bible school in Los Angeles, I was walking by a city park and saw a young Hispanic man wearing the attire of a gang member. The Holy Spirit spoke to me and said, "If you ask that guy to accept Christ, he will say yes." After arguing with myself—*that can't be the Lord's will . . . this guy is a gang member!*—I decided to obey anyway and struck up a conversation. I happened to have a Spanish edition of the Four Spiritual Laws in my New Testament. After talking with him for 15 minutes, to my utter surprise, this tough-looking teen prayed with me to accept Christ!

That young man's immediate response represents the exception rather than the rule. In my early Christian life, if people didn't respond to the gospel, then I would apply my standard motto: "Increase the pressure!" Frankly, that approach to evangelism resembles a practice used by many cults called "love bombing." Great attention is given to prospective converts for four to six weeks—supposedly as a means for showing love. It often turns out to be a fake love, just a sales tactic to convince newcomers to join. If someone refuses, he or she is dropped like a hot potato.

God relates to each person we contact as individuals. Our call to share the good news means loving people until they come around to relationship with Jesus Christ—regardless of how much time it takes. Those who don't give the Holy Spirit adequate time to do heart surgery will hinder His role of ripening the seeds we may have helped to plant. Our job is to bring them the love of Jesus with all the grace He provides.

WHY DOES SERVANT EVANGELISM WORK?

I believe servant evangelism works because it respects certain important factors that influence the effectiveness of evangelism in our society. Let's consider these key factors one by one.

Sharing the Good News Is Not a One-shot Deal

American Christians tend to view evangelism as a one-shot deal— a "let 'em have it while we've got their attention" blast from both barrels of a shotgun loaded with Scripture. Sharing the good news of Jesus Christ with our neighbors is a *process* rather than a *project*. Like people everywhere, those joggers in Houston were on their own journey toward or away from God. Some were already friends with God, some were alienated children, and others were already well on their way to discovering God.

Paul states, "I have planted, Apollos watered, but God gave the increase" (1 Cor. 3:6). Implied in his words is the notion of evangelism as a process, a sort of spiritual continuum that includes every human being. Paul's view of evangelism is quite unlike our American mindset that tends to focus on the "harvesting" aspect of soul winning rather than the planting part.

Opening hearts that have long been closed to God's love is not something that normally happens quickly. Dr. Paul Benjamin discovered a common pattern after interviewing hundreds of people who had come to Christ in the early 1970s. In his book *The Equipping Ministry*, he states that the average person requires five significant encounters with the gospel before accepting Jesus Christ as Savior.[1] Dr. Benjamin defines a "significant encounter" as one in which a person actually *hears* the message of God's love in such a way that it registers in his or her heart. We see in this conversion pattern that it is one thing to *send* a message and quite another to see that message make a lasting impact on someone's life.

American Christians tend to view evangelism as a one-shot deal—a "let 'em have it while we've got their attention" blast from both barrels of a shotgun loaded with Scripture.

I can remember at least five significant encounters that led to my own decision to receive Jesus as Lord and Savior. First, after attending a Doobie Brothers rock concert, someone handed me a tract about God's love. Even though it was poorly written, the Lord used that brief message to get my attention. Not long afterward, a second touch occurred when I noticed that a barber had put a before and after photo of himself in his storefront window, along with a sign claiming that Jesus had made a difference in his life. Third, I picked up an issue of *Time* magazine that covered the story of the Jesus People movement in Southern California.

A fourth experience came in high school when I nearly drowned at a lake in Northern Arizona. I had heard that drowning victims see their life pass before them. Mine did. That experience scared me enough to focus my attention on questions of life, death, eternity and God. Not long after I began to ask these questions, I met a couple of Christians who told me their story of coming to Christ. And not long after that fifth touch, I asked Jesus to enter my heart.

My own experience underscores my belief that the lion's share of bringing the good news involves the planting and watering of seeds of love through simple acts of kindness. We must be willing to plant and water before we will begin to see the harvest.

The first 90 percent of bearing witness to God's love is "pre-cognitive." The Holy Spirit is doing a deep work in the *heart* of the person being drawn to the Lord. It is not so much a matter of sharing *information* as sharing *love*. We often plant these seeds of love long before people have consciously considered the claims of Christ. The Holy Spirit—the "Hound of Heaven"—is always busy doing a deep work in the human heart long before a person can give language to God's action.

Anyone Can Do Simple Acts of Kindness

For most Christians, doing evangelism is a lot like going to the dentist: No one really enjoys doing it, but it has to be done every once in a while. They often equate "being obedient to God" with doing something that is distasteful, unnatural, and even contrary to their nature. In other words, if preaching at the park scares me to death, it must be God's perfect will!

Some of those who went to the park in Houston admitted later on that they went along just because they wanted to "obey the Lord." When they switched from preaching to simply offering relief from the elements to those who jogged by, every person on the team felt encouraged. They realized this was something they could do easily. Failing at an assignment like this is almost impossible. Worst case scenario: The Popsicles melt because people aren't hot and thirsty enough.

I've found that people are often more comfortable *doing* for others than they are simply *talking* to them. In fact, the reported number-one fear of Americans is talking to strangers! When they assume they're being asked to do the very thing they most fear in life, it's no wonder so many Christians cringe at the prospect of evangelism.

On the other hand, serving is a reasonable task to ask of the average "coward" in the Body of Christ. I believe that most of us are cowards when it comes to sharing the gospel with strangers. When using these simple approaches to touching others, timid Christians come to realize they have nothing to lose. That's a good feeling.

---

*For most Christians, doing evangelism
is a lot like going to the dentist: No one really
enjoys doing it, but it has to be done
every once in a while.*

Servant evangelism is a low-risk venture. It doesn't take a great deal of gifting, money or even boldness to influence large numbers of people. For several years, we looked for simple ways to influence shoppers at local grocery stores, a natural gathering place for many Americans on Saturday mornings. During the winter, we regularly gave away fresh brewed coffee. We found that it was easy to attract people from our church to participate in this kind of project. After all, who *can't* pour a cup of coffee?

Doing Acts of Kindness Is "High Grace"

When we stepped out to do simple deeds of love, God usually showed up to bless our efforts. His presence was often tangible. Time and again, we saw Him convert our simple acts of service into powerful and unforgettable seeds planted in people's hearts.

During the Christmas season, we provided free gift wrapping at several area malls as a part of our outreach efforts. Our refusal to accept money shocked many of our customers who were used to paying for everything. One afternoon, a couple of volunteers were manning our wrapping booth when a woman brought in a couple of presents. As they wrapped her gifts, they explained to her that they were doing this to show her God's love in a practical way. This woman asked if we were the kind of Christians that believed in "healing prayer." When they answered yes, she asked if they would pray for her back. She explained that she was a flight attendant and had been off work for some weeks due to a lower back problem. With a mall full of people walking by, they prayed a simple healing prayer. After a few moments, she noted with an amazed look that her lower back was completely numb. The pain had completely gone away.

Sometimes God's grace appears in a powerful sort of way, as with the flight attendant. At other times He is present in more subtle ways, as with the joggers. Whenever we serve, each person is influenced in some unique way by the personalized touch of the Holy Spirit. Instead of telling the gospel in a forced way, we simply answer the questions others initiate.

Evangelism Hits Home When It Begins with Acceptance

Houston, Texas, is sometimes called the "Buckle of the Bible Belt." The prolific number of churches in that city prompts people to think of it as a bastion of conservative Christianity. To those outside the scope of the Church, however, conservative Christianity is not always seen in a positive light. In fact, they often perceive believers as resembling Dana Carvey's "Church Lady" on *Saturday Night Live*.

One skit centers around a church potluck supper where a single mom apologizes to the pastor for the small dish that she has to offer. He tells her, "Whatever you can bring is good enough for this dinner." Moments later the Church Lady arrives carrying an elaborate casserole that everyone makes a fuss over. She points out to all present that she spent hours preparing this dish. Because it is so enormous, the single mom feels inferior. In her mind, the Church Lady had scored because everyone has once again recognized that she is better than most people. The skit ends with the Church Lady doing her "superior dance," strutting about with her head bobbing and her hands on her hips. The American public finds this character funny because she embodies the way many outsiders perceive Christians.

Some of the joggers in the park may have perceived the preaching group as pushy, judgmental, self-righteous and rejecting of others who didn't think exactly the same way. When we use the phrase "the *Bible* says," we don't necessarily get the immediate attention of the world, and we certainly don't get their immediate respect.

For centuries Christians have been identified through a variety of badges that vary from one culture to another. At times they have been known by the length of their hair (or lack of hair), crosses around their neck, wearing plain clothing or dark garments, getting rid of their TVs, or avoiding certain foods. All of those "signs" are cultural identifiers, statements to their particular generation about their own personal faith.

According to the Bible, only one true and lasting sign identifies us as followers of Jesus through all times and cultures. The world around us recognizes the same sign that Jesus pointed to: our love. "By this all men will know that you are my disciples, if you have love for one another" (John 13:35, *RSV*). This love must spill over from the walls of our churches and out into the community in significant ways if we are going to make any lasting impact. It seems people don't necessarily remember what they are *told* of God's love, but they never forget what they have *experienced* of God's love.

We cannot love people without first accepting them. A group of young people from our church has been reaching out for several years to the patrons of an alternative dance club in the downtown Cincinnati area. Those who regularly attend this club present a scary appearance with their shaved heads, tattoos and black leather clothes. One young guy named Paul was amazed that Christians would polish his black boots for free just to demonstrate the love of God. He began to spend time with this group of Christians and eventually came to church with them.

It seems people don't necessarily remember what they are told of God's love, but they never forget what they have experienced *of God's love.*

When these Christians first met Paul, they were unaware that he had been convicted of a crime and was weeks away from starting a four-year prison sentence. While serving time, Paul began to consider the actions of these Christians. He felt like he had encountered real love because they seemed to love him as much as they loved one another, even though he wasn't a believer. That seed of kindness—which began when his boots were shined for free—sprang up after several months of confinement when Paul asked Jesus Christ to enter his life. Hearing about God's love was important to him, but the power of acceptance proved to him that God's love is real.

Evangelism Must Overcome a Credibility Gap

We live in a day when the Church's credibility is at an all-time low. When we step up to bat in sharing the good news with the unchurched public, we already have two strikes against us. Billy

Graham saw the world's summary of the Church during an anti-Vietnam rally some years ago when a student held up a sign that read, "JESUS *YES!* CHURCH *NO!*" Even today, that slogan accurately reflects the feelings and attitudes of many people across our country.

Because of the front-page publicity given to sex and money scandals involving several visible leaders in the Church, many unchurched people feel Christians must earn the right to be heard. Before we share God's *words* of love with a hurting world, we must first be willing to do *deeds* of love with the heart of a servant. We must balance the speaking and the doing of the gospel—the words and the works of God—if we expect to gain an audience with the watching world.

In our attempts to share the gospel, many of us have talked a lot but been weak on demonstration. John Wimber makes this important point in his book *Power Evangelism* when he says, "Jesus both spoke the *words* and did the *works* of the Father."[2] We need to become word-workers, as Wimber encourages.

Mother Teresa brought clarity to the world's viewpoint in this statement: "True acts of love go before God forever as worship to him." Instead of just telling the gospel, we are *bringing* the gospel to people. Our society expects to be preached at by enthusiastic Christians. It is almost shocking to unbelievers when we break that expectation by offering simple, practical demonstrations of God's love.

People often asked us, "Why are you *really* doing this? You want me to join your church, don't you?" Typically we responded with, "You're sure welcome to come to our church, but more than anything we are here because this is the way Jesus walked on the earth. If He were bodily walking the streets of Cincinnati today, Jesus would be showing people the love of God in practical ways. Instead of washing feet, He might be washing cars. After all, that's the way people get around these days."

An Experience of Love Opens a Person's Heart
to a Message of Love

A group of Christians traveled to the summer Olympics in Barcelona hoping to do significant evangelism in the large crowds gathered from around the world. Unfortunately, they received less than an enthusiastic welcome from the local officials who informed them that evangelism was specifically not allowed. Instead of reacting negatively to this message, this group of believers went to work meeting whatever practical needs they saw. They began to clean up the streets, empty trash cans, and generally do whatever they could see that needed to be done around the Olympic grounds.

After a few days of watching these Christians, the officials called the Christian leaders in and admitted that they were pretty impressed with the attitude that they had seen displayed. They went on to ask, "What sort of evangelism were you hoping to do, if you were allowed?" After the Christian leaders explained themselves, they received the okay to pursue whatever outreach they wanted as long as they kept in touch with the civic officials. What a staggering turnaround, and all because these believers were willing to *be* the good news before they began to *speak* the good news.

Who answers God's mail? Joe and Jared's experience makes it clear that He wants to involve us in the process. God answers His own mail, but He does it through people like you and me, people who are willing to step out and touch others through simple demonstrations of His love. I now see myself as one of the carriers of the Lord's mail. You and I have been called to be a part of God's conspiracy, a conspiracy of kindness aimed at the heart of every person alive today. The easiest entrance point into someone's life is a simple deed done in kindness. In the next chapter, let's look at some of the barriers to getting involved in this conspiracy of kindness.

More Kindness

I think of life as an opportunity to move among the people who God so loved that He gave His only Son to die for them. I have not always seen people that way. I began to pray some years ago, "God, give me a love for people that allows me to see them the way You do." While I am naturally an introvert, He has gradually answered that prayer over the past couple of decades. He is giving me a concern for people that works like this: My internal "radar" is on more often than it is off. When I am around people now, I usually pick up on what is going on with them.

I am now, despite my natural introversion, at a point of being willing to engage people in conversation. I look for things I might have in common with them. Maybe it is something they are wearing, something they are carrying, the coffee order they placed. There are literally hundreds of signs each person has hanging around his or her neck that are openings for me to engage—if only I will pay attention. The question is, *Am I looking for the signs?*

Look, and then step out. There is nothing to lose.

Like me, you will find that once you begin to converse with 99.9 percent of people, they are hungry for conversation. They are for the most part lonely and even desperate for friendship and belonging. Our call as Jesus-followers is to be available to fling our seed of care and simple conversation. In the middle of that natural way of behaving, it is common that the "extra natural" happens.

These God opportunities are common for those of us who have joined the conspiracy of kindness. It is not anything spooky. It is as simple as can be. And it begins with the art of noticing—noticing what people are going through, then noticing what God says we can do to partner with Him in showing love in a practical way.

Notes
1. Paul Benjamin, *The Equipping Ministry* (Cincinnati, OH: Standard Publishing, 1977).
2. John Wimber with Kevin Springer, *Power Evangelism* (San Francisco: Harper & Row, 1986, 2000).

CHAPTER 2

Unlearning the "E" Word

The heart that breaks open can contain the whole universe.
JOANNA MACY

I taught at an elementary school for two years before I began pastoring full-time. One day while my fourth-grade class was playing softball, an enthusiastic boy named Lloyd decided his team would be more likely to win if he were to trip the base runners as they came by. When I caught him sticking out his foot, I benched him for the remainder of the game.

Lloyd was so upset that he called me a few names. "You're nothing but a dirty—," he mumbled under his breath so that I couldn't quite catch the word. He wouldn't repeat what he had said to me, so I invited Lloyd to an after-school conference with Mr. Ferguson, the principal—a man who was widely feared among the fourth-graders.

Lloyd was still too embarrassed to tell us what he had said. We insisted he come clean and got him to tell us the first letter. Lloyd said it began with an "e." Mr. Ferguson and I looked at each other and silently mouthed, "What terrible curse word begins with an 'e'?" Again we pressed Lloyd to tell us.

"Okay," the boy said, "I called Mr. Sjogren a dirty little *idiot!*" ("ediot," depending on how you spell it). For the rest of that school year, the staff often asked me if I had been called the "e" word lately.

Some words have a tendency to take on an emotional edge after a while. Every so often it's important for us to examine the redefinitions that may have quietly taken place. For example, when many Christians hear the word "prayer," they don't feel encouraged. Rather, they feel like failures. Just about every Christian I know finds it difficult to carry on an effective prayer life. After years of personally struggling with prayer, many of us assume that everyone else who loves Jesus is doing great in that area. Soon the mere mention of the word "prayer" sets off intense feelings of guilt.

"Evangelism" is another one of those emotionally charged words that often send shivers of guilt running up and down our spines. It registers in us emotionally the way Mr. Ed the talking horse would have said it in the 1960s, with a little vibrato: "Eee-vannnn-gelllll-issssm-uh!" So many of us feel like failures when we try to share our faith—all but the few who can really do it well. That may be the way we feel, but it's not supposed to work that way. Somehow along the way we've become confused about what it means to represent Jesus to the lost world around us.

So many of us feel like failures when we try to share our faith—all but the few who can really do it well.

Everyone agrees that evangelism involves giving away the message of God's love. We agree on the *focus* of our message, but diverge greatly when it comes to deciding *how* that message is to be carried to the world. When I was a new Christian, I was influenced by a confusing hodgepodge of books, tapes, radio Bible teachers, and enthusiastic friends, and blindly adopted others' values as my own. As a result, I had a rocky start in evangelism.

My attempts at sharing the gospel could be divided into three phases: the "shark phase," the "carp phase," and finally the "dolphin phase." (These helpful terms were coined by authors Dudley Lynch and Paul L. Kordis in their book *Strategy of the Dolphin*.[1]) Let's examine the way that Christians typically approach evangelism in light of these three possible choices.

THE SHARK

Sharks don't just live life; they attack it! They come at life with great aggressiveness, with control as their highest value. Sharks tend to be movers and shakers who love to take over any project at hand. They're known for getting a lot done but not necessarily without incident. On the downside, sharks tend to traumatize everyone around them with their unfettered aggression. Consequently, they don't always have strong long-term prospects for productivity. Sharks tend to fit the picture of all the worst characteristics of a pushy salesman.

Most of what we think of as "personal evangelism" falls under the shark approach. If we were to conduct a word-association test on the average American using the word "evangelist," I believe we would get some telling responses. Many Christians unconsciously take on a certain persona when it comes to doing evangelism. Having become used to an image, we may no longer be sensitive to elements in our behavior that keep unbelievers away from God.

Even though stereotypes of evangelists may be exaggerated, they are often grounded in the truth. Comedians who appear on late-night talk shows often pick up on this caricature. They portray those doing evangelism as angry, pushy, loud (when loud isn't necessary), opinionated, militant, Southern-accented (even if from Des Moines), sweaty (frequently dabbing forehead with monogrammed, white handkerchief), someone who can make a two-syllable word out of a one-syllable word ("Gaaaa-duhhh" for "God"), unreasonable, negative (emphasizing the judgment of God), and simplistic in their thinking (black-and-white terms that are overgeneralized).

This description fit me to a T at an earlier point in my Christian life. From the first day of my conversion, I wanted *everyone* to meet this Jesus who had transformed my life. I began to do evangelism without the aid of any books or teaching. The only model I had was one provided by the older people who attended local holiness prayer meetings: hold meetings, give testimonies, and call people forward to give their lives to Christ.

After being away at school for a year, I was picked up at the airport by my mom. In the course of the one-hour trip home, I eagerly explained to her everything I knew about the entire message of the Bible from Genesis to Revelation. I was talking so fast that I must have sounded like an auctioneer. All Mom could say was, "And it's nice to see you again too, Steve." It must have been difficult hearing a teenager explain the meaning of life.

I spent the first several years of my Christian life seeking to "soul win" everyone in sight. During this time I lived with the view that the world was a very disorderly place. As I saw it, my assignment was to bring it into order by evangelizing. I cornered every relative and friend who would listen for a few minutes and let them have it with both barrels. It wasn't long before I had shell-shocked everyone I knew. After a while when people saw me coming, they would make up excuses like, "I can't talk now, I've got to polish my dog."

Looking back, talking with me must have been as exciting as going to the dentist. What I shared during that time was the truth, but the package in which the message came wrapped was incredibly unloving and insensitive. At that time I was in actuality functioning more as a *soul alienator* than a *soul winner*.

I wouldn't leave home without a handful of tracts. I especially enjoyed putting them in unusual places—like menus in restaurants, magazines in the store racks, even in a roll of toilet paper for the next person in the restroom stall to read! My favorite tracts capitalized on the use of fear to get people's attention. One had a picture of a hearse on the front and read, "You put your own shoes on this morning." Then it read on the inside, "But tonight the undertaker may be taking them off."

After a while when people saw me coming, they would make up excuses like, "I can't talk now, I've got to polish my dog."

The goal of the shark's approach to evangelism is confrontation. Once I was out with a group of my friends doing what we called "street witnessing." We would walk up to total strangers and try to share the good news with them. As soon as I had said the words, "Hi, I'm a Christian and I'd like to talk with you for a few minutes," one man turned around and spoke to me while facing in the opposite direction. He said, "I'm going to count to 10. When I finish if you're still standing behind me I'm going to give you a black eye." That was my idea of giving away God's love.

After five years of enthusiastically offending people for the Lord, I could see the fruit of my efforts all around me: I had traumatized most of my friends, relatives and neighbors. I told myself I was being rejected because I loved God so much, but my victims didn't see any love at all in what I'd done. I had managed to ostracize all of my family and friends in the name of the Lord. Even so, the aggressiveness of the shark model seemed to me to be the only possible gear for bringing Christ to non-Christians. (I think it might be wise to send all new Christians to a remote desert island for the first couple of years of their Christian life to work out their faith and temper their enthusiasm with a measure of wisdom.)

THE CARP

At the opposite extreme of sharks, carp move through life in a lethargic manner. They see themselves as life's victims, too weak to ever function as a change-agent in life. Carp exist on the bottom of the river and live off of food that the other fish have discarded. They have the opposite nature of the aggressive shark. Carp are dropouts from the fight and make it their primary aim in life to seek the safe route and to avoid any sense of responsibility. Carp don't *make* things happen; they *watch* things happen around them and seem to never have any clue as to why life goes as it does.

In terms of evangelism, carp are sometimes former zealots for the Lord, believers who have become discouraged along the way and have given up trying to lead others to Christ because they couldn't take the pressure. These former sharks usually don't consciously decide to take a break from sharing the good news. Many simply don't understand that there is more than one way to bring God's love to the world. Their love for God or people hasn't necessarily grown dim; they've just grown tired of militant evangelism.

I once spoke with a pastor who had heard about the basic idea of servant evangelism. Wanting to do something unusual for his community in California, he decided to sponsor a free, no-donations-allowed car wash. At that time, a severe drought kept water at a premium, so the pastor had to buy the necessary water. He and a couple dozen people from the church washed more than 100 cars. In conversation after conversation, the drivers were stunned at this simple act of love.

At the end of the day, the workers gathered to share about various encounters with people from the community. As they did so, this pastor began to weep. He realized that in one three-hour period, he had shared the good news of Jesus Christ with more people than in the previous two years combined! I have known this pastor for several years. He is a man with a great love for God and a strong desire to bring people into the kingdom of God. But like many Christians, his life had been carpish for some time. Without a workable model, he was stuck watching the world go by rather than intersecting it with the love of Jesus Christ.

THE DOLPHIN

Dolphins combine the strengths of sharks and carp. These people are enthusiastic and positive about life, yet keep the issue of personal responsibility in proper balance. The dolphin moves through life with a deep sense of purpose, whereas the shark tends to be overly responsible and the carp accomplishes little or nothing. The dolphin has a mission in life, but still has fun on the way to the goal.

In recent years I have sought to live more as a dolphin—proceeding with a clear objective in my evangelism but also seeking to enjoy life along the way. My new motto is, "Where the Spirit of the Lord is, there is fun!" Deep down I have always been a dolphin. I believe most of us are really dolphins, but when we begin to act like sharks, our message becomes difficult to believe.

At Vineyard Community Church, we worked to teach the youth from our church about approaching evangelism as dolphins. During one weekend conference, along with several other churches from the Cincinnati area, the 1,000-plus teens and their leaders went out to do personal evangelism. The youth groups showed up unannounced at a large local mall and began to do shark-like evangelism—all of the groups except for the teens from our church. Our youth leaders held back when the other groups dispersed into the mall. They waited to see what needs people might have and then simply tried to meet those needs. The group soon went to work carrying shopping bags, picking up trash on the ground, emptying ashtrays, and cleaning storefront windows for merchants.

When mall personnel asked why they were being so helpful, they responded with our usual reply: "We just want to show you God's love in a practical way." Several lengthy conversations were started with curious bystanders. Before long an irate customer called the police to complain about the more sharkish evangelists. As our youth quietly went about serving in practical ways, the police escorted the other youth groups out to the parking lot.

I believe most of us are really dolphins, but when we begin to act like sharks, our message becomes difficult to believe.

As I look at the Gospel accounts of the life and ministry of Jesus, I can see that He went from person to person operating as a dolphin. He modeled for us a life that balanced times of intensity with periods of relaxation. Jesus clearly understood who He was and what His call from God entailed. No Scripture better captures His call than the reading from Isaiah 61, which served as the text for Jesus' first sermon, probably spoken at the synagogue where He had grown up.

Those who had watched Him grow up were now seated in front of Him as Jesus was handed the scroll. "The Spirit of the Lord is upon me, because he has anointed me to preach the gospel to the poor. He has sent me to heal the brokenhearted, to preach deliverance to the captives and recovery of sight to the blind, to set at liberty those who are oppressed, to preach the acceptable year of the Lord" (Luke 4:18-19).

Jesus' audience didn't like what they were hearing. The ministry He described was so different that the synagogue leaders, a predominantly sharkish bunch, became furious. These verses describe evangelism according to Jesus. He *knew* His audience: the broken. They came with different kinds of brokenness, but they all needed God's love in order to be healed. Jesus also knew His approach: simple and direct. In short, *Jesus was a bringer of God's love to the broken of the world.* That's evangelism, Jesus-style. We are called to bring the good news to the world in just the same way.

THE OLD VERSUS THE NEW

A friend of mine played high school football on one of the most successful teams in Southern California in the 1950s. One of the keys to their success was the way their practice sessions always began on Monday afternoon: with a review of the goals of the game of football. After some warm-up exercises, the coach would call the players to the middle of the field for a basic overview—and I do mean basic. He would start out holding up a football and saying, "This is a football. Notice the shape, feel, size and color. The object of this game is to carry this ball across the goal line at the opposite end of the field. No points are awarded for running backward or sideways." This award-winning coach would carry on like this for the first few minutes of every Monday's practice. Any player who laughed or didn't pay attention had to run laps as punishment.

Most Christians who set out to do evangelism fail to define their goals beforehand. And not knowing the goal makes it difficult to succeed. For the most part, the contemporary Church still uses models of evangelism from a different century. I don't believe it's necessarily true that "old" is bad and "new" is good, but I do think our evangelistic efforts often operate on the premise of "the old is good and the new is suspicious." Many Christians resist new wineskins, including new ways of bringing the gospel to the world. Vance Havner, the often-quoted pastoral statesman, maintains that the last seven words of the Church will be, "We've never done it that way before."

Traditional models for evangelism typically focus on the special gifting of a few visible evangelists. Anointed communicators such as Jonathan Edwards, Billy Sunday and R. A. Torrey have played a vital role in bringing the message of Jesus' love into the world. These approaches were very effective at various points in Church history, but the society into which the gospel must be spoken has changed tremendously. The outward form of any approach is useful for a season and then eventually wears out. We need to have the insight to retire those methods that have completed their lifespan.

The early days of William Booth's Salvation Army offer a good example of the amazing effectiveness of a type of evangelism that worked at one time but no longer suits modern society. In the latter half of the 1800s, the Salvationists were able to draw in massive crowds from the London streets with marching brass bands. Once the crowd had assembled, open-air preaching would win many to Christ.

A few years ago, I visited Oslo, Norway, where I saw a group of enthusiastic people marching through the streets and calling people to an open-air meeting. What I saw was nearly exactly the same approach that was used some 100 years ago. What worked as a cutting-edge approach to preaching the gospel in 1850 brought little or no response in Oslo that day.

A review of Church history reveals predictable patterns in the way groups develop. A particular five-step pattern has been repeated many times. A *man* (or woman) captures something fresh from the heart of the Lord. That person's obedience and application of truth cause *methods* to emerge. As those methods are applied on a broad scale, *momentum* builds. That momentum grows stronger and stronger until a *movement* emerges. After the person who founded the movement dies, the white-hot presence of the Lord eventually cools down. The group continues on, unaware that their methods have lost effectiveness. After all, the movement is still intact and the methods still produce some results.

Typically, groups find it difficult to be completely honest about a loss of momentum. They tend to spiritualize what is happening: "The Lord must be teaching us something in this season of unfruitfulness." Of course, the Lord probably is indeed teaching them something, but the group may be operating in a universe of their own making, which doesn't require an objective reality to continue. Existing church machinery can become self-perpetuating. The focus shifts from what the Lord *is* doing to reflecting on the glory days—what the Lord *was* doing. Monuments are established, books are written, and the founders become posthumous heroes in the afterglow of what happened "once upon a time."

The focus shifts from what the Lord is doing to reflecting on the glory days—what the Lord was doing.

This five-step cycle suggests that leaders tend to see what they want to see. The Church as a whole often loses sight of the modern world. We forget how the people of our generation hear the Christian message. The gospel of Jesus Christ is unchanging, but the trappings of the world around our message are ever-changing. In just the same way, the heart of our evangelism remains constant, but the exterior stands in need of continual change in order to communicate effectively to contemporary society.

We need to ask some searching questions regarding how we approach evangelism in this generation. I suspect that if William Booth were alive today, he would be doing things a little differently than he did a century ago. Many Christians have fallen in love with methods and paid too little attention to results. Jesus warned the Pharisees that they were incapable of seeing the new work of God because they were emotionally involved with the old "wineskin," the old way of doing things. We too need to constantly examine our wineskins. Unchecked, we tend to perpetuate ways of sharing the gospel that may actually undermine our message.

LEARNING WHO WE ARE

Some ill-fitting programs resemble David's efforts to put on Saul's armor when he first headed off to face Goliath. King Saul was trying to help David emerge victorious over Goliath, when David had a pretty good idea of how to handle the situation nicely. This shepherd had already killed a lion and a bear. The giant, he reasoned, would fall just like those wild animals he'd encountered in the past. David had to use the approach to battling Goliath that suited him rather than listen to eager scriptwriters who wanted to give him half-baked advice on how to take down giants.

Let's be ourselves. Let's give ourselves to God for Him to use. In the end that's all we can offer to Him. Now that I've stopped trying to be someone I'm not, I've been making some discoveries about who I am. When I aspire to simply be myself, the Holy Spirit's presence is most effectively released through me. My desire isn't to imitate someone else's Christian life, but to be the unique child of God He has created me to be. That discovery has changed the way I communicate the good news to those outside the church.

Sometimes we share the gospel with little verbal explanation. Some of our projects require even little or no direct contact with those we are serving. We have found that these acts of love and service are strong enough to stand on their own without any conversation about God. For example, a woman had parked her car in downtown Cincinnati while she went shopping. One of our teams that feeds parking meters saw that her allotted time was about to expire, put a quarter in the meter, and attached a flyer with our logo at the bottom and this message:

> While you were gone we fed your parking meter to show you God's love in a practical way. If there is anything further that we can help you with, please call us at 671-0422.

This woman was so impressed with this deed of kindness that she called an AM radio talk station with the largest audience in this part of the country. She explained to the radio audience what had happened and wondered aloud, "What kind of people would do something like this for others they don't even know?"

The talk-show host followed up by interviewing us over the phone. At several points he said, "You don't *really* do this stuff, do you? You're kidding me, right?" He picked up on the fun element in what we were doing. We took him out with us the following Saturday. We had one team giving away coffee in the downtown area, another was washing windshields, still another group went around feeding parking meters. He went along with the group that was cleaning toilets in area restaurants. Every restaurant manager was shocked when we asked if we could clean their toilet for free, no donations accepted. One manager's response was classic: "This sort of thing hasn't been done in hundreds of years. You people are like monks or something."

Seeing the World Through Jesus' Eyes

After realizing that I had listened more to the scriptwriters than
to my own heart, I began to examine my own values. I found
it a very helpful exercise to ask myself, "How did Jesus go about
His ministry as depicted in Scripture?" I have since made a conscious effort to adopt these values as my own in every area of
my life, including evangelism. Here are some observations of a
script according to Jesus, a man who was the same on the outside as He was on the inside.[2]

- *Jesus saw through the eyes of the kingdom of God.* Like the
  frontline troops of an army advancing to reclaim lost
  territory, we are bringing the kingdom of God to bear
  in this life. Jesus was committed to establishing
  beachheads in Satan's territory. He was committed to
  raiding the camps of darkness and setting free the men
  and women being held captive. As we wait and look
  for Jesus to come and win the final battle, our primary
  call is to evangelism.

- *Jesus saw through the eyes of Scripture.* Our desire is to
  do and teach simply what the Bible says. Its message
  holds power when it is read and believed just as it is,
  without imposing any presuppositions and precon-
  ceptions onto the text. We must also go beyond
  knowing the message of the Bible to obeying it.

- *Jesus saw through the eyes of mercy.* Ours is neither to make
  names for ourselves nor to build lasting institutions,
  but to meet the needs of broken people through a
  ministry of mercy. The church is the place where righ-
  teousness and mercy meet.

• *Jesus saw people through the eyes of simplicity.* The Son of God did nothing for religious effect. Rather, He operated in a natural, low-key manner.

• *Jesus saw people through the eyes of integrity.* It is vital that what we say is the same as what we do. We must always be careful to speak the truth, deal honestly, and live uprightly.

• *Jesus saw people through the eyes of His culture.* Jesus had the ability to speak the cultural language of His day so that people could understand His message of God's love. We too need to help others see how the gospel can be relevant to their everyday lives.

• *Jesus saw people through the eyes of reality.* Jesus walked in the Spirit and recognized the supernatural works of God. He functioned equally well on a rational plane in His teachings. He both brought and explained the power of the kingdom of God.

Jesus admits the secret of His success: "The Son can do nothing of himself, but what he sees the Father do" (John 5:19). If we are to succeed in bringing the good news to those around us, we must place our expectation for success in the right place.

PRESSURE POINTS

For my first five years as a Christian, I mostly spoke the good news but lived out something very different. Later, because of confusion about how to approach evangelism, I moved away from actively sharing my faith. If someone went out of his or her way to ask me about the Lord, I would offer some explanation, but I wasn't obeying the clear call of Scripture to "do the work of an evangelist" (2 Tim. 4:5).

I had confused *my* role and *God's* role in the evangelism task. Seeing myself as the evangelist, I saw it as my responsibility to bring people into relationship with Christ. During those first five years, I had approached evangelism as a high-pressure activity—with the majority of the pressure placed on me. Most of the time, I was feeling personally guilty for not being more successful. Having created a common double bind, I felt bad about not being more effective in leading others to Christ, but whenever I did try to do evangelism, I would take on unbearable responsibility for the outcome. Sheer guilt even motivated me to witness sometimes.

---

*I used to feel that a person's coming to
know Christ was a direct result of my efforts.
I saw myself as the one delivering others
to God's doorstep.*

My confusion stemmed from looking to models who were the most gifted, the most mature, the most extroverted members of the Body of Christ. The people who have been effective in evangelism tend to be the ones who write and speak on the subject. These people tend to be strong personalities, sharks as I described them earlier in this chapter.

No matter what our approach to sharing the good news, we will be forced to put pressure on one of these four sources:

1. Pressuring the Christian who is evangelizing
2. Pressuring the person who is being evangelized
3. Pressuring the evangelism program
4. Pressuring God

I believe that most of our evangelistic efforts have falsely put pressure on the first three, while failing to place our trust squarely on God's shoulders where it belongs. We have pressured everything that can be pressured except God. Yet He not only allows us to pressure Him, but He also even invites us. One of my favorite invitations is Jeremiah 33:3: "Call to me, and I will answer you, and show you great and mighty things, which you do not know."

We will never know many things until we begin to see our perpetual lack of wisdom apart from God's intervention in our lives. Zeal for God can be a wondrous weapon if we walk in the attitude Jeremiah suggests. Unfortunately, we often forget the source of all wisdom and strength and attempt to go it alone when we approach evangelism. I used to feel that a person's coming to know Christ was a direct result of my efforts and that I was obligated to get him or her to make that decision. I saw myself as the one delivering others to God's doorstep.

Besides pressuring myself, I was also prone to putting pressure on the program. I was looking for the ultimate outreach plan, one that "really worked" at bringing others to Christ. Almost any approach to doing evangelism will get the attention of Christian leaders because so many of them keep their focus fixed on the program. I don't believe that *any* approach contains the secret for effective evangelism since no program can withstand the pressure of our expectations.

In my attempts to evangelize, I would also put pressure on those hearing the gospel, usually in the form of fear, which I swung as an ax over their heads. Many times I would prematurely push people to pray regardless of how they felt or what they understood. Once I had engaged people in a conversation about God, I would always ask them before leaving if they wanted to accept Christ. Many who teach on evangelism present this practice as something positive. I now believe that this is often an inappropriate and untimely question to blurt out to an unprepared stranger. On the many occasions I succeeded in getting a stranger to pray a sinner's prayer with me, I wonder how many did so just to get me off their back.

My sentiments were echoed in a videotaped interview I saw with Fr. Rick Thomas, a Catholic priest from El Paso, Texas. Fr. Rick works with the poor of Juarez, Mexico, just across the border from El Paso. His flock literally lives in the junkyard. As he talked about his ministry to the poor, Fr. Rick said, "We can't *share* the 'good news' and *be* the 'bad news' at the same time. It doesn't work." In a moment of personal soul-searching, I saw that I had communicated God's good news in a bad-news way and probably done more damage than good for the cause of Christ on Earth.

"Christians and non-Christians have one thing in common: They both hate evangelism."

If we don't carry the pressure for success in evangelism on our own shoulders, and if we don't place pressure on the hearer or on the program, where should our expectations rest? Where they should have remained from the beginning: on God. Our misplaced expectations will ultimately result in great frustration. In fact, all of our sins and failures can be traced back to our human tendency to find other sources instead of God to meet our needs.

The Westminster Confession states, "The Holy Spirit . . . is the only efficient agent in the application of redemption. He regenerates men by his grace, convicts them of sin, moves them to repentance, and persuades and enables them to embrace Jesus Christ by faith. He unites all believers to Christ, dwells in them as their Comforter and Sanctifier, gives them the spirit of Adoption and Prayer, and performs all these gracious offices by which they are sanctified and sealed unto the day of redemption."[3] In short, the Holy Spirit is the only true evangelist who has ever existed. His is the only power in the universe that can turn a convert into a disciple who looks like Jesus Christ. If the Holy Spirit truly is the only evangelist who has ever been, then we are free to remove pressure from the wrong places. We can begin seeing ourselves as coworkers with the Holy Spirit, letting Him do what only He can do anyway. Our role is to *enjoy* the flow of God's life through us as we share our joy with others. When we abide in God, we don't just speak or even demonstrate the message of His love; we *embody* that message in a way that makes people stand up and take notice.

When we first approached a local mall for permission to do free gift wrapping at Christmas time, many of the store managers thought we were a bit odd. I went to three interviews during which I was grilled at length about what we were *really* up to. They wanted to know word for word what we were planning to tell people when we wrapped their presents. The primary manager (who happened to be Jewish) was convinced that Christians could do only two things well: take offerings and preach. When we offered to serve with no strings attached, we caught him off guard. Expecting a shark, he didn't know what to do when he caught a dolphin.

Finally, the management group agreed to let us wrap gifts, but with the stipulation that if anything unauthorized happened they would close us down without notice. When we passed their tests with flying colors, they raved about the success of the project and invited us to return again the following Christmas. We went on to wrap presents for several seasons, and with each passing year we received more favor from the mall owners. They even began to give us multiple locations and lots of advertising visibility, and they purchased all of the wrapping materials for us.

It seems that the fear of the "e" word is universal. Many of us have experienced firsthand the truth of Rebecca Pippert's observation when she says, "Christians and non-Christians have one thing in common: They both hate evangelism."[4] Slowly, as we go about the city giving away both the works and the words of God, we see a growing openness of heart. Christians are becoming bold in an authentic way. Outsiders are wondering why we are showing them so much care. Most importantly, God is building a work force to bring His love to hearts that haven't yet been touched.

MORE KINDNESS

Since the release of *Conspiracy of Kindness*, I have spent a lot of time interacting with evangelism architects from around the world.

I still stand by the principle that all evangelism is good evangelism. On the other hand, it is up to us to think like professional golfers when they make the selection of their clubs. We have to make the right "club" selection. Now, I am not much of a golfer. In fact, I have not played in more than a decade. But this much I know: When in a sand trap, it is not very useful to draw out a putter!

Keep this in mind: We are professional gatherers. This idea is so important it is worth the price of this book (whatever you paid for it!). It is essential that we keep a gatherer mindset before us continually in life. Jesus said we are fishermen. Fishermen don't think in terms of going out to catch a fish here and there every month or two. No, they cast gigantic nets and don't concern themselves with the kinds of fish they are after. They are in love with *catching*—not fishing!

We can't control all factors. Not by any means. But we can keep on showing up and leave the results to God, just as any pro fisherman does. If we continue to show up—if we continue to throw our nets into the water and pull them out with our boat at high seas—we will catch fish. It really is that simple.

Jesus said that this is the age of catching. This is the age of the harvest. There is an abundance of opportunity. If we open our eyes, we will see what is before us. Let's keep on keeping on.

Notes

1. Dudley Lynch and Paul L. Kordis, *Strategy of the Dolphin* (New York: Ballantine, Fawcett Columbine, 1988).
2. Jack Simms, John Wimber, Dave Workman and Steve Sjogren contributed to these observations.
3. Douglas F. Kelly, Hugh W. McClure III and Philip Rollison, *The Westminster Confession of Faith, An Authentic Modern Version* (Signal Mountain, TN: Summertown, 1979).
4. Rebecca Manley Pippert, *Out of the Saltshaker and Into the World* (Downers Grove, IL: InterVarsity Press, 1979), n.p.

CHAPTER 3

Low Risk, High Grace

Our deeds determine us, as much as we determine our deeds.
GEORGE ELIOT

One of the drawbacks of doing kindness evangelism in Cincinnati is the weather. We often went through weeks of poor conditions such as rain, snow, sleet, severe cold and tornado watches. The old saying is true: "If you don't like the weather in the Midwest, just wait. It'll change shortly." Many of our initial projects required reasonably sunny weather. After all, who wants their cars washed in the rain?!

To deal with the unpredictable climate, we came up with several all-weather projects. My favorite one was cleaning toilets. Stop and think about it before you reject this idea. Toilets are plentiful—at least one in every home and business. Most of them are in need of at least a little cleaning. And almost anyone can clean a toilet, even someone like me who suffers from a weak stomach. Unpleasant smells, sights and even noises send me in the opposite direction. When my mom heard I was cleaning toilets for strangers, she commented, "*Steve* is cleaning toilets? That proves there is a God in heaven!"

On one ministry outing just before Christmas, we sent several groups into one of the nicer parts of town. Some were cleaning toilets at businesses and restaurants. Our approach was simple and direct: We usually walked up to the person in charge and said, "Hi, we'd like to clean your toilet for free." After they picked themselves up off the floor, they usually said something like, "I could have sworn you just asked me if you could wash my toilet for free, but I know that can't be true. No one has ever cleaned our toilet for free."

On this particular day, a Christmas party was in progress at a well-known restaurant and bar. They seemed to be having a good time eating, drinking and carrying on. While one of our teams was working in the restroom, a doctor came in who had been drinking a bit too much. When he asked why they were there, they explained themselves. This man told them he too was a Christian but was unfortunately in a compromising position that day. It wasn't long before he asked the team to pray for him—right there in the men's restroom! They reported that the doctor did most of the praying, asking God to touch his life and renew him in his Christian walk. I would like to have been a mouse in the corner listening to this man explain to his wife later how his Christmas party went!

This story illustrates one of the primary benefits of servant evangelism: It combines *low risk* with *high grace*. Every ministry venture involves an aspect of both risk and grace. In order to be successful, we must live within the limits of our emotional, financial, spiritual and relational budget, so to speak. As I see it, very few church leaders have a good grasp on the cost of projects before they leap in with both feet. If secular businesses operated that way, most of them would have gone bankrupt long ago. Let's examine how these factors of risk and grace affect the area of evangelism.

THE RISK FACTOR

Jesus referred to the risk element of the kingdom of God in this parable: "What king, going to make war against another king, does not sit down first and consider whether he is able with ten thousand to meet him who comes against him with twenty thousand? Or else, while the other is still a great way off, he sends a delegation and asks for conditions of peace" (Luke 14:31-32). Jesus evidently considered this king wise for counting the cost before venturing into battle.

Many attempts to share the good news rate high on obedience and enthusiasm but low on careful consideration of what we may be getting ourselves into.

Every outreach carries a price tag, whether that cost is readily evident or more hidden. Some costs are easy to measure; some aren't. Many attempts to share the good news rate high on obedience and enthusiasm but low on careful consideration of what we may be getting ourselves into. What are some of the risks involved in bringing the good news to those who need to hear it?

Relational Risk

First, we must consider the relational risk. Let's say that I step out as a leader and tell others that we're going to have "big fun" by knocking on doors. Take it from a veteran door-knocker: The average Christian will have anything *but* fun. If I gather and train an evangelism group from my church with this kind of promise, I will have eroded my credibility as a leader. I would be guilty of underestimating the relational risk of that particular outreach. The next time I invite these same people out to have "fun," they will all think twice about whether or not they can stand that much fun in a single morning.

Financial Risk

Some evangelistic approaches are very expensive. Some time ago a large crusade was held in Cincinnati with a number of positive results. Numerous churches that didn't normally associate with one another came together in unity. Many lay people were trained and encouraged in their personal evangelism techniques. And many people came forward and made a profession of faith, in addition to those who made a decision to rededicate their lives to the Lord.

But by the time the choir had finished singing the last hymn and the evangelist had packed his bags for home, the downside of this outreach became evident: the enormous cost. For a week-long crusade, the total price tag amounted to well over $1 million! I myself received letters for nearly a year soliciting funds to cover the remainder of the debt. I think all the churches that participated in this crusade were pleased with the results, but I don't believe anyone realized how much hard work would be involved in paying off the bills. Perhaps the organizers would have thought twice if they had literally counted the cost of the crusade beforehand.

Emotional Risk

The emotional risk is probably the greatest cost to consider. As a borderline introvert, I personally need to do projects that don't require a lot of interaction with strangers. Going door to door is a traumatic experience for most people because of the enormous rejection rate. One friend recently confided in me that he was often so afraid of being rejected that he would pray that no one would be home when he went door knocking in his efforts to start a new church. He would sometimes have to just stop for the day because he could take no more dissenting voices. And this man is the gifted pastor of a nationally known church. If this experienced minister struggled with talking to total strangers, what does the average Christian do? Yet the most popular approaches to bringing the good news require huge emotional risks.

At one time I regularly went out with a Christian group that is well-known for its confrontational style of street witnessing. The first time I went out with them, they gave me a police whistle along with a pile of tracts. "So what's the whistle for?" I innocently asked. They responded, "Sometimes people get pretty mad at us for giving out tracts and talking on the streets. Every once in a while one of us gets attacked. If you do, just blow the whistle and we'll know you're in trouble and come running."

Now that's how I spell R-I-S-K.

Spiritual Risk

Finally, evangelism entails a spiritual risk. Whenever we seek to win someone to Christ, we raise the ire of the Evil One. Satan is not one bit happy when people escape his grasp and start following Jesus. Carriers of the good news become, to some degree, walking targets of the enemy. The spiritual reality behind our practical efforts must be prayerfully taken into account when we aspire to do evangelism.

In light of all these risks, it's no wonder the word "evangelism" so often instills fear in us. Unfortunately, our leaders have done much to perpetuate this fear by not balancing the risk with the available assets. If we hope to present a picture of evangelism attainable by the average Christian, we'll have to rediscover the grace of God to meet the risk.

THE GRACE FACTOR

It's one thing for people to show up to do evangelism, but is the Lord also going to show up when we arrive? Scripture assures us that God is present with the believer wherever he or she goes.

We have His *abiding* presence, but I have experienced a *ministry* presence of the Holy Spirit that seems to ebb and flow.

Matthew made reference to this reality in describing Jesus' visit to His hometown of Nazareth: "He did not do many mighty works there because of their unbelief" (13:58). As one who has shown up to do ministry when the Lord stayed home, I can assure you that it's no fun being out there without the immediate presence of the Holy Spirit. If we take an honest look at the typical evangelistic efforts that are being used in most of our churches, we can see that many of them actually require very little of God's active blessing in order for the program to keep rolling forward. Such attempts at sharing the good news will inevitably prove ineffective in the long run.

It's one thing for people to show up to do evangelism, but is the Lord also going to show up when we arrive?

As the Son of God, Jesus had high expectations for God's ministering presence to be upon His every move through life. I believe God still heals, but many pastors believe differently. One of their primary objections to the healing ministry comes in the form of a question: "If God still heals, then why don't you just go down to the hospital and begin praying for cancer patients from bed to bed?"

I receive that question as coming from a sincere heart, but anyone asking it doesn't understand that the ministering presence of God does not remain at the same level each time we pray. And it wasn't that way for Jesus either, as pointed out in the Matthew 13 verse. So why did Jesus see so many people healed when He prayed for the sick? The answer lies in the fifth chapter of John, which describes how Jesus healed a man at the pool of Bethesda who had been ill for 38 years. How did He pick out this one man from a "multitude of invalids, blind, lame, and paralyzed"? All of them needed healing, but the Lord touched only one that day. Jesus explained, "Most assuredly, I say to you, the Son can do nothing of himself, but *what he sees the Father do*; for whatever he does, the Son also does in like manner" (John 5:19).

Jesus experienced an enormous success rate in praying for the sick because He prayed only for those He saw the Father touching and healing. The Son pursued only the "high grace" cases, the ones the Father pointed out. Praying for the sick simply meant *noticing* the ones the Father was already touching, then *identifying* that touch, and *blessing* it to be done.

Successfully bringing the good news to others requires involving ourselves in projects that require the presence of the Lord. Our motto must be, "If God shows up, everything is going to be fine. If He doesn't show up, nothing much is going to happen here." I have a pastor friend in the Baltimore area who has learned to walk in that mindset. He felt for some time that God wanted his church to become involved in outreach at the local high school. When he approached the school on a number of occasions to ask permission, those in charge graciously replied, "You know, we just can't mix church and state. We can't officially allow you on campus. Sorry."

Some time later this pastor relayed his frustrations to me in a conversation. I suggested that he consider doing an outreach off campus but still close enough to touch significant numbers of students in short spaces of time. A few weeks later he pulled off his first outreach—a huge success! About a dozen folks from his church set up a folding table at a corner near the high school and offered the passing students a free soft drink.

Over the following weeks this same team gave away popsicles, cassette tapes with Christian music and buttons with the slogan "I love you—J.C." Before long this church was touching three to four hundred students at a youth meeting every Friday evening. My friend later related this story to me and said, "You know, it's amazing what a can of Coke along with God's presence can do. It can open a human heart to God's love!"

CHOOSE YOUR QUADRANT

The elements of risk and grace suggest a variety of possible combinations in reaching out to others. Some of the choices are livable only for "Super Hero" Christians. Others are workable for your basic chicken who loves the Lord. It is important that you find the quadrant that fits you best.

Risk
What is the cost:
emotionally?
spiritually?
relationally?
financially?

Grace
How much of God's presence
is necessary for this outreach
to be a success?

Low Risk Low Grace	High Risk Low Grace
High Risk High Grace	Low Risk High Grace

Low Risk—Low Grace
Low-risk evangelism may be attainable by the average Christian, but I don't want to ever be involved in an outreach project that doesn't require God's presence in order to succeed. One popular approach in starting a new church involves randomly calling large numbers of people and inviting them to attend. While that program has been successful on occasion, I have heard far

more failure stories. There's not much risk involved for the person making the phone calls, but there's not much supernatural working of the Spirit of God either. This past year I have received several of these phone calls myself. In the most recent invitation to attend a new church in Cincinnati, the person was calling from Michigan!

Some might say, "Some outreach is better than no outreach." Perhaps so, but I feel that if God is not clearly present in our projects, then we are wasting our time by essentially trying to flog a dead horse. Jesus promised that we could do nothing without Him, but with Him we would bear much fruit, fruit that would remain (see John 15:5,16). As we hunger for a greater measure of His presence and grace, we are assured that we will bear much fruit in sharing the good news of God's love.

High Risk—Low Grace

Hogan's Heroes, a popular television comedy from the sixties, repeated a common phrase in nearly every episode. If Sergeant Schultz messed up one more time, his superiors threatened to send him to the dreaded "Russian Front," an actual place where the warfare was so intense that very few came back unwounded. Unfortunately, a lot of the outreach projects I have been involved with over the years fall into this "Russian-front" category.

Unfortunately, a lot of the outreach projects I have been involved with over the years fall into this "Russian-front" category.

Of the four possibilities, the high risk-low grace quadrant is most likely to discourage people from doing evangelism if they continue in that vein for long. These kinds of outreaches also cause the outside community to label Christians as fanatics. In short, we're talking about an approach that is costly and will not yield much return. That sounds like the description of a couple of cars I've owned!

On numerous occasions I have gone with groups knocking on doors to share the gospel. This approach is high risk because we are invading the private space of people, that special place called home. Fifty years ago, when most Americans lived on farms, people might have welcomed such visitors, but not anymore. This approach is low grace because it puts the primary pressure for results on the person sharing the gospel.

Door-to-door evangelism usually entails explaining the gospel and then systematically answering someone's questions. The belief is that if we can adequately answer their questions and objections, then they will logically come to the Lord. In this approach, the person with the quickest mind and the best grasp of language skills usually makes the best evangelist.

My own experimentation with a number of approaches to evangelism has indicated that they all work to one degree or another. The one exception to that rule has been the survey method. Perhaps you yourself have been surveyed at the mall or in the parking lot of a sporting event. This approach disguises the evangelist as a research interviewer who requests information in order to put the interviewee at ease. The survey starts with simple, safe questions.

First we ask, "How long have you lived in this community?"

We move on to, "Do you like living in this community?"

Then we touch on personal tastes, "Is your car American-made or an import?"

Finally, we move in for the kill with, "Would you say you have a personal relationship with Jesus Christ or not?"

Christian researcher George Barna has awarded the survey approach with the Millstone Award in special recognition for a ministry practice that impedes the gospel in America.[1] Clearly this approach is deceptive. We gain the trust of those we're interviewing and then—BAM!—we spring it on them. Just when they were getting relaxed in the conversation, the Christian trying to share the good news shows that people who love Jesus are not to be trusted and in fact may be out-and-out hypocrites.

Earlier in my Christian life I participated in a long string of high risk-low grace outreaches. I guess I had a high capacity for failure. For example, I attempted several evangelistic Bible studies during college. I'm fairly good at talking people into things they aren't interested in doing, but this approach challenged even my sales skills. The idea behind this approach is to invite several nonbelievers to your dorm room for an hour of Bible study. The study of God's Word is always powerful and worthwhile, but getting people to attend is a difficult trick to pull off.

I believe high-risk approaches to sharing the good news can be effective in certain settings. I liken sharing the good news to playing golf. The rules of this game allow 13 different clubs to be carried in the golf bag, each one appropriate at some point in the game. At the beginning of each hole, the goal is to drive the ball as far as possible down the fairway. For that shot a wood club is appropriate. Getting the ball on the green usually requires an iron club. A putter is best for the final goal of sinking the ball into the cup.

Imagine a golfer making the claim, "I'm committed to just using my putter. I'm a putting specialist. I have a whale of a time getting from the tee to the green, but once I'm within 50 feet of the cup, watch out—I'm deadly!" It would be equally ridiculous to think of a golfer using only a wood for his entire game.

Evangelism works the same way. We need an entire "golf bag" full of approaches for reaching those in our communities.

Though many of the traditional approaches to sharing the gospel are rather high risk, they have proven to be effective over the years. We would be committing an error in judgment to drop every other approach to evangelism just to adopt servant evangelism. I vigorously support any approach that effectively encounters the unchurched. My hope is that we can grow in our effectiveness by growing in our diversity, that we can learn how to draw on the appropriate "club" at the right time in bringing the good news.

I believe high-risk approaches are particularly effective in the final phases of the evangelism process where people are making a personal commitment to follow Jesus. These same methods often come up short when we focus on them to the exclusion of others. When we have only one means for sharing the good news, we will surely limit our effectiveness in evangelism.

High Risk—High Grace

Ventures in this category include "power evangelism," foreign missions and starting a new church, all of which center around the direct confrontation of God's kingdom and the kingdom of the Evil One.

The term "power encounter" aptly describes the spiritual warfare that takes place when God's presence collides with the powers of darkness in the lives of the lost. The manifest presence of the Lord and powerful gifts of the Holy Spirit convince unbelievers of the reality of God. Such ministries are exciting and make for goose-pimple stories, but they are not for the faint of heart. Each of these approaches carries a high requirement for God's presence in order to succeed.

Power evangelism begins when God sovereignly releases His power by giving someone supernatural insight into another person's life. This approach is a bit tricky, first because we cannot manufacture those insights from the Lord. Only God can initiate prophetic encounters. I believe God desires to speak in these ways, but my experience is that He doesn't do so with great regularity.

Second, every human being remains subject to error, even when the Lord does speak. After moving in the gifts of the Spirit for years now, I still proceed with great caution when I sense the Lord has shown me something about another person. I am acutely aware of the possibility of my being mistaken. My opening words are usually, "I may be wrong, but I think the Lord is saying this . . ." I am a frail human who has tens of thousands of thoughts going through my head every day, only a few of which are inspired by the Lord.

The high-risk element of power evangelism is obvious. It takes tremendous courage to walk up to a total stranger and tell him or her what you sense the Lord is saying. In fact, it takes more courage than most pastors have, not to mention the members of the flock following their leadership. When I first began hearing from the Lord in this way, I thought the day would soon come when most of my church would be experiencing a significant level of spiritual gifting. I thought it would be commonplace to hear dynamic healing stories. I was wrong. I naively thought the average Christian would be more courageous than I have found to be the case.

Having something to *give* seems to open the door for significant conversation. Fear on both sides is diminished once we enter into an encounter with a simple deed of kindness. These acts give us the baby steps we need to gradually walk into others' lives. With each step, a little more courage seems to come our way and we grow steadily in our ability to interact with nonbelievers. When a divine appointment is set up by the Lord and we happen to be His spokesperson, we need lots of courage to step out and be bold.

Fear on both sides is diminished once we enter into
an encounter with a simple deed of kindness.

We noticed that as we were serving others, we sometimes became aware of a current difficulty they may be facing—a sort of spiritual sensitivity from the Lord. One morning, we were going door to door in a middle-class, black neighborhood on the north side of Cincinnati offering to wash the windshields of the cars parked in the driveways. The people of this neighborhood had always been receptive to us, if not a little amazed at the notion of white men going door to door in a predominantly black area. This particular Saturday, Dan, a new believer and member of our church, was with me.

We came to a house where a woman was talking on a princess-style phone with a long extension cord. She put the phone down momentarily after we rang the doorbell and asked what we wanted. We explained our project and got busy cleaning the three cars in her driveway. As we were finishing up, the conversation between Dan and me shifted from the current state of Reds baseball, to politics, to—out of nowhere—the clear sense that this woman had recently been divorced and was barely hanging on to her sanity.

My first thought was, *Boy, am I a judgmental person! Why am I thinking these thoughts about this nice lady?* A moment later, God showed me further that this woman had two teenage children who were giving her fits. I sensed that the combination of her ex-husband and children was driving her to the edge of her ability to cope, but that God wanted to touch her in power.

It's one thing to have a sense that you may be *getting* something from the Lord, but a completely different challenge to actually *share* what you think the Lord is saying. The words we receive will carry an impact only if we use great wisdom in knowing how to share that spiritual insight. In this case I was operating more in faith than in great confidence. My heart began to thump loudly and I felt a little dizzy. With little polish, I went to the door and knocked. When the woman put her hand over the phone and thanked us for washing her windshields, I boldly stepped out on a limb and asked her, "By the way, have you recently been divorced and are your kids driving you crazy?"

The woman's reaction to my question was amazing. She immediately burst into tears and hung up the phone. If we devised a scale for rating tears—with a level one being a slight trickle and a level five being weepy, this woman was sobbing at a level nine. Her tears were leaping out horizontally!

My friend Dan didn't know what to think. I didn't know what to think. I certainly didn't expect this sort of reaction to my question. We both felt a little embarrassed at this encounter. All we could think to pray was for God's mercy to come to this lady. After a few minutes the shaking and weeping gradually subsided. Betty, as we found her name was, then asked how we knew about her situation. "I don't know anything about your situation," I said. "The Lord just spoke to me as I was washing your windshield."

On another occasion I took a group out in Birmingham, Alabama, to wash windshields at a shopping center parking lot. One woman, who had expressed fear of going out with the group, was washing the windshield of an empty car. As she did she noticed an infant car seat and had a strong impression that the baby who sat in that car seat had recently been very ill. She felt so moved that she prayed a simple prayer for the baby, just in case her sense was correct.

Just as she finished washing the windshield, a woman approached the car with a grocery cart. This woman expressed thankfulness for the clean windshield and began to load her groceries into the trunk. The woman from our church had a clear sense that she ought to offer to pray for the baby. Mustering all the courage she could find, she blurted out, "Has the baby that sits in that car seat been deathly ill lately?"

With that the mother burst out weeping, saying, "Yes, my baby almost died recently. How do you know so much about my baby?" The woman who had timidly stepped out to wash windshields got much more than she bargained for: instruction as to the proper use of a squeegee as well as a word of knowledge that opened the heart of a stranger struggling with pain and fear.

When power encounters do happen, they make our job as bringers of God's love incredibly easier. The drawback is that none of us can cause a prophetic insight from God to come to us. I can't cause anyone to be healed or touched by the presence of God. My only hope is that God in His sovereignty will come and touch the needy, and hopefully allow me to be a part of that encounter.

We saw a lot of healings over the years, but they seemed to come in spurts. I don't know why, but we seemed to go through seasons when these encounters were common and then long stretches when they almost didn't happen at all. As far as I can tell, our hearts were equally open from meeting to meeting, but the evidence of God's power in our midst seemed to be ever changing.

In some ways I see power encounters and servant evangelism as "kissing cousins." They both work on the basis of disarming a stranger by demonstrating God's immediate presence. The person is enabled to see the power of God—whether that be accomplished by a free Coke or a word of knowledge that reveals hidden thoughts and emotions. Both acts can be equally powerful in demonstrating God's love. But beyond that common element of making an entry point by showing God's immediate presence, the two approaches diverge greatly. Receiving words of knowledge when doing kindness evangelism remains the exception in our experience.

Low Risk—High Grace

I believe that this is the best area for most Christians to explore in reaching out to others with the good news. Servant evangelism is low risk in that it doesn't require a lot of money, time, expertise or emotional energy to be effective. It is high grace because we carry out this ministry with simple honesty toward God. "God, if You are upon this project, something of significance will happen. But, Lord, this is just a simple service we're performing. We know that nothing of lasting value will be imparted here unless You are upon us."

More traditional high-risk approaches ask people to do more in evangelism than they are capable of doing. We have, in a sense, set the high jump bar at seven feet, a height that only Olympic-level athletes can clear. Expectations for results have been set at an impossible emotional height for most Christians. One look at the task and most of us shake our heads. I know I could never pole vault seven feet. My only hope for looking good would be to cheat and use a hidden trampoline for extra oomph!

After a while, the consistent theme of rejection and failure overwhelms the average Christian. Eventually, most of us just throw up our arms in frustration and quit. We become carp: sitting on the bottom of the river and sucking mud, but at least we're safe. We become victims of a faulty conclusion that says, "There must be something wrong with me and my walk with the Lord because I really don't enjoy doing evangelism."

No matter how many clever ways we use to prop up our approach to evangelism—"new and improved" programs, videos, books and seminars—nothing much is going to change until we alter the basic proposition. Unless we can lower the risk and raise the sense of God's presence in our encounters, the average Christian will continue to see evangelism as something only experts can do. Thank God for the experts, but I don't think that's what God intends. Evangelism doesn't have to be that way. I have been learning to walk free from the sense of guilt and fear in evangelism by minimizing the risk and maximizing the need for God's grace. Low risk and high grace fit together nicely.

Eventually, most of us just throw up our arms in frustration and quit. We become carp: sitting on the bottom of the river and sucking mud, but at least we're safe.

FROM PRAGUE TO FORT WORTH

I spoke one summer at a gathering of several dozen churches in Prague. I was slated to speak twice, once to a smaller gathering of pastors and later to the entire group of several thousand. After speaking to the pastors, there was a lot of discussion as to whether they felt good about my presenting this approach to evangelism to the larger group. The leaders weren't sure they agreed with the approach I described. With some reluctance, they agreed to have me share with the larger crowd. Afterward I invited any interested people to come out the following morning to do a few kindness evangelism projects.

I was only prepared for a dozen or so, but to my surprise, a couple hundred people showed up! When I saw the number of participants, I sent someone to the store to buy chewing gum. Gum is inexpensive there, so for about $50 we were able to buy several thousand sticks. For several hours we had gum teams going about the streets of downtown Prague. We had also purchased in advance enough windshield washing tools to equip several teams.

When the group re-gathered to share their experience, I sensed enormous excitement in the air. They were excited because, in the words of one man, "this is something anyone can do." As the stories of that day trickled in over the next few weeks, the leadership group grew more and more excited. I was invited back to speak another summer to a conference of 2,000. The leaders wanted to take all of the attendees out into the city and do outreaches at 40 or so locations around Prague.

While speaking at a Bible school in Fort Worth, I commented that low risk–high grace outreach succeeds easily. For the most part, the group was made up of veteran Christians who had long ago grown accustomed to high-risk evangelism and ceased seeing new opportunities for carrying the good news to the world. They had gotten used to an insurmountable high-jump bar and thought that's just the way evangelism happened to be.

I challenged those gathered by asking how many of them had recently interacted with someone outside the church. I was not surprised to find that only 1 or 2 percent of them responded in the affirmative. This group, like many veteran Christians, had created an unrealistic image of evangelism. That high risk–low grace picture caused them to live in a very confined universe that was nearly 100 percent full of just Christians.

I challenged this group to find new ways of experimenting with lower-risk approaches to getting out of the church and into the community. With a marker in my hand, we brainstormed for a few minutes. Being unfamiliar with the area, I didn't know what we could spontaneously do in that part of town. After a few minutes of discussion, we decided to go to a laundromat located just 100 feet from the front door of the school, where we would put quarters into the washing machines for customers as they walked in.

The students asked me what the proper technique for doing this was. I told them just to watch me. Little did they know that I had never done a laundromat outreach—I was figuring out how to do this as I went along! With several students peering over my shoulder, a mother with two kids in tow walked in with a huge pile of laundry. When I saw which machine she was planning to use, I put quarters in the machine and simply asked, "Do you want hot or cold water?" She answered with a little surprise in her voice, "Cold. Why do you ask?"

"We're a group of Christians doing a community service project to show God's love in a practical way. We want to pay for your wash this morning just to demonstrate God's love to you."

As you might imagine, this lady had lots of questions. I asked one of the female students to answer her questions and help her fold laundry. Thirty minutes later I left the laundromat. All around the place the students were connecting with the people who had come in to wash their clothes. Some were engrossed in conversation; others were laughing and telling stories. The first woman we helped was quietly praying and weeping with the girl who had stepped out to help her.

When I spoke again at the school the next day, I opened by asking the students who had gone to the laundromat to share their perceptions. One young guy began to tell what happened and broke down crying. He said, "I saw God really touch lives yesterday. And to think that in just a few minutes we were able to get into their lives, just by feeding some quarters in the washing machines. I never thought it could be this easy bringing God's love to people."

THE DISCIPLES STARTED WITH LOW RISKS TOO

In His three-year ministry, Jesus spent most of the early days with the disciples showing them how to do what He did. From the early pages of the Gospel accounts, we see Jesus actively taking risks. He was casting out demons, preaching the message that the kingdom of God was at hand, miraculously feeding large numbers of people, even raising the dead on occasion.

Most of the three years Jesus was with the twelve, the action revolved around Him. Then gradually, step by manageable step, He imparted ministry opportunity to the apostles. When He fed the four thousand (see Matt. 15:32-38), the disciples' job was to carry the bread and fish from Jesus to the people. Afterward, they picked up the mess. That was a manageable risk. Later, these men were sent out for just a few days to do some of what they had been watching Jesus do. They too cast out demons, healed, cared for and fed others, and preached the arrival of God's kingdom (see Luke 9:1-6). It wasn't until much later, after Jesus had returned to the Father, that the disciples began to do apostolic works similar to those done by Jesus.

We don't have to have all of the answers a non-Christian might ask in order to make a significant impact.

The kingdom of God is sown in the hearts of growing and maturing disciples bit by bit, manageable risk by manageable risk. Of course, all of us can tell a story or two about having to step out of our comfort zones occasionally in order to make progress in our Christian lives, but generally we need to proceed at a more conservative pace. We need to first learn how to jump an attainable height before we move on to the next slightly increased level.

The Christian life is meant to be simple rather than complicated. One does not need to be a mature believer to perform acts of kindness. In fact, a brand-new believer can effectively do this sort of evangelism. We don't have to have *all* of the answers a non-Christian might ask in order to make a significant impact.

One Friday evening before Labor Day, rush-hour traffic was backed up for nearly a mile at the corner where our church is located. The temperature was 95 degrees with a matching humidity level. About 10 of us from the church quickly went into action to touch several hundred hot, frustrated motorists with God's love. We iced down 400 soft drinks and set up signs just down the road: "Free Drinks Ahead."

As the drivers approached the stop sign, we would ask, "Would you like diet or regular?"

"Diet or regular what?" came the skeptical reply.

"We're giving away free soft drinks to show people God's love in a practical way."

"But why?"

"Just because God loves you."

Reactions varied greatly. Some people smiled, some shook their heads, several mouths dropped open. Most were a little stunned to receive something for free. A United Parcel Service driver drove away saying, "But I don't even know you guys. Why would you do something like this for me?"

In less than an hour, we had given out all 400 Cokes. We had spoken with about 600 people (some didn't take a Coke but wondered what we were doing), and we even made the local radio station's helicopter traffic report. While we were cleaning up afterward, one man commented, "This was so much fun I don't know if it even counts as 'evangelism.' " Another guy standing nearby responded, "I don't know if it is evangelism, but it'll do until the real thing comes along!

Whatever we did, a lot of people experienced the reality and love of God this afternoon."

Just as with the apostles, Jesus is patient with our growth. He knows that most of those who represent Him and His kingdom will be around for a long time to come. Perhaps some of us will be singled out to participate in special high risk-high grace activities, but I believe most Christians are meant to dwell in the realm of low risk-high grace. Regardless of our quadrant, God is intent on our reaching a place of maturity in His kingdom where we will be consistently carrying His life to a world that is dying for lack of His presence and love.

More Kindness

Have you ever prayed a prayer that you later regretted praying? I have. I have prayed and then gone back to God to ask Him to cancel out that prayer, if He would be so kind.

More than once, I have told God that I was ready to give up on scattering His seeds of kindness because I had had enough. I have had "Jonah moments" every now and then—when I saw the enormity of the call, felt emotionally overwhelmed, resisted and ran!

Not long after *Conspiracy of Kindness* was released, I spoke at a church in Colorado about living outwardly and with an open hand, about giving without an expectation of a return, as Jesus did. When I finished, a man approached me. He was middle-aged and had a big, black Bible. He didn't look out of place in the least. He said, "I want to shake your hand!" So I obliged him. Then he went on to say, "Now I can tell people that I have shaken the hand of the dumbest guy on the planet!"

He told me that anyone who lived a life based on the principles I had laid out in my talk was a complete idiot! To give one's life away and not expect anything in return was lunacy. I reminded him of a couple of Jesus' well-known sayings, such as "It is only in losing your life that you find your life" (see Matt. 16:25; Luke 9:24), yet the man had a completely different spin on each of those verses. After going round and round for a while, I finally told him, "God bless you, bro—but you are in a very small percentage of people who read those verses and see them the way you do!"

It is antithetical to human nature to be available to give of ourselves. We are by nature completely selfish. But when Christ comes in, something elemental changes. When the early believers were called "Christians" (literally, "little Christs"), it was their generosity toward others that was being highlighted. Through Christ, God builds a new nature into each of us little Christs, a new way of being that desires to make others more successful at every level than ourselves. That is God's power flowing through us.

Note
1. George Barna, "Ministry Currents," January-March 1992 (Glendale, CA: Barna Research Group).

Beyond Us and Them

Man stand for long time with mouth open before roast duck fly in.
CHINESE PROVERB

Imagine going through several days at a parachute training school where the teachers had covered every phase of successful jumping. The students learned how to select the right parachute and how to pack it, even the importance of color coordinating one's jumping apparel. They had studied great parachutists of the past, read accident statistics of those who had failed, and then simulated jumps. Finally, the training ended, the tests were graded, and a graduation ceremony was held to acknowledge all those who had passed.

As the president of the school spoke about its long and proud heritage, everyone was happy—except for one student. Although it was out of place right in the middle of their celebration, he raised his hand. When the speaker asked what was wrong, this one student meekly stood up and said, "I feel silly getting a certificate showing that I'm qualified to parachute. I haven't actually jumped out of an airplane yet."

With that everyone in the room turned, gasped simultaneously, and sternly replied, "Don't you know, we don't *parachute* anymore. We just study and talk about parachuting!"

I have experienced much the same attitude in being trained to do evangelism. As a student at a fine Bible school in the Los

Angeles area in the mid-seventies, I joined many other young people from unchurched backgrounds. We had all experienced profound conversions to Christ in and around the Jesus Movement that was then flourishing in Southern California. The students, who were new to Christ and placed little value in church-related traditions, combined with the faculty members, who had known Christ most of their lives, made for a combustible mixture.

In this fertile environment I soon became involved in the "evangelism team," a group of about a dozen people who met for three hours every Friday evening to do evangelism. Early in the school year, we all experienced great enthusiasm for going out to share God's love with nonbelievers. Even so, it seemed only appropriate that we first adequately prepare before venturing out. We read several books on the topic, saw some films, had lively discussions about how we could most effectively evangelize. We even did role-playing as a way to practice sharing our faith.

Eventually Christmas vacation hit and we hadn't yet finished our training time. School resumed and—you know how time passes quickly—before we knew it, spring break was upon us. About the first of May, it dawned on me: the "evangelism team" should have been called the "preparation team." We really didn't do any evangelism. What we really did was talk, pray and train for evangelism. Our group never did go out into the community that year.

One Friday evening toward the end of the year, I made that observation to the leader of the team. He patiently responded in a patronizing way, "Steve, I love your enthusiasm, but we just aren't ready to go out yet. When you get older in the Lord, you'll see the wisdom in what we have done this year." I was being told that later, when I grew more mature in Christ, it would make sense that the "evangelism team" really didn't do evangelism. I didn't get it then, and I still don't get it.

I operated as a sort of Christian agoraphobic:
loving the Lord, but afraid to go outside
the house of the Lord.

I've spent most of my Christian life being stuck in these kinds of fears and myths about life. I operated as a sort of Christian agoraphobic: loving the Lord, but afraid to go outside the house of the Lord. In recent years, however, I've been venturing out of the Christian ghetto that once kept me bound. I've been saying no to the fears and myths that once gripped me and kept me in a place of inactivity. To put it another way, I've been daring to color outside of the lines.

THE KINGDOM: THEORETICAL OR PRACTICAL?

Our Wednesday night services were geared mostly toward believers so that we could spend a longer time in worship and encourage the practice of the gifts of the Spirit. I began to notice a man who usually attended. It was hard *not* to notice Willy—he was six feet five inches tall, had a blond mohawk and dozens of tattoos covering both arms. His most evident tattoo was a frog imprinted on the side of his head. Whenever I'm near Willy, the eyes of this frog seem to be looking at me no matter where I stand. When I first questioned Willy about his regular attendance at our meetings, he responded, "I can feel something here so I come and listen to the songs you sing."

Willy once showed me that he had been featured in *Tattoo* magazine. Until then, I didn't even know such a magazine existed. When I asked him what he did for a living, Willy answered, "I buy and sell things." My sense was that it just wouldn't be appropriate to ask him exactly *what* he bought and sold.

I tried to build bridges with this guy even though we were from incredibly different worlds. I don't have a single tattoo and I wear polo shirts and khaki pants. Maybe I didn't make a lasting impression on this man, but I nevertheless feel good about trying to step out of my comfort zone and into a very different life circle to show God's love to Willy.

Like the parachuting school, it seems we don't *do* evangelism so much as we talk about it. For the most part we are satisfied just studying the good news. A multitude of fears and myths regarding *us* as Christians and *them* as non-Christians often keeps us from sharing the gospel with those in our community. I must admit that I was afraid of Willy. My friends in Bible school were afraid of reaching out. Fear seems to be a cruel theme in our lives—one that keeps us from doing what God has called us to do.

Jesus tells a story of three men who were stuck in the same kind of fears (see Luke 10:25-37). While two of them continued in their fears, one made a bold escape. Jesus was asked by a lawyer in the crowd, "What shall I do to inherit eternal life?" Jesus' answer was essentially, "It's very practical. Love God and love your fellow man." The man, wanting to minimize his level of responsibility, asked, "Who is my neighbor?" Jesus replied with the parable of the Good Samaritan:

> "A certain man went down from Jerusalem to Jericho, and fell among thieves, who stripped him of his clothing, wounded him, and departed, leaving him half dead. Now by chance a certain priest came down that road. And when he saw him, he passed by on the other side. Likewise a Levite, when he arrived at the place, came and looked, and passed by on the other side. But a certain Samaritan, as he journeyed, came where he

was. And when he saw him, he had compassion on him, and went to him and bandaged his wounds, pouring on oil and wine; and he set him on his own animal, brought him to an inn, and took care of him. On the next day, when he departed, he took out two denarii, gave them to the innkeeper, and said to him, 'Take care of him; and whatever more you spend, when I come again, I will repay you.'"

Jesus then asked the lawyer, "Which of these three do you think proved to be a neighbor to the man who fell into the robbers' hands?"

The lawyer replied, "The one who showed mercy toward him."

And Jesus said to him, "Go and do the same."

Jesus' answer to the question "Who is my neighbor?" was, in brief, "Your neighbor is the person right in front of you with a need in his or her life." No matter what those people look like, even if they happen to be our natural enemies, we are called to show them the love of God.

In other words, the way we (the Church) treat them (the unchurched) serves as a litmus test of our spiritual health.

Jesus tells us that the way we treat others displays the condition of our hearts. In other words, the way *we* (the Church) treat *them* (the unchurched) serves as a litmus test of our spiritual health. The three men in the parable were offered the same test: What to do about a man beaten to the point of death and left lying in a ditch? None of them were aware at the time that they were taking a test; only one passed by responding to the need placed in his path.

Frankly, most of my Christian life has resembled the actions and attitudes of the priest and the Levite who walked right past the wounded man. Let's take a closer look at these two men who had separated themselves from the world, people who were held in a vise by the same fears that affect you and me.

The priest and the Levite saw God's kingdom as a *separate* kingdom. They saw the law of the temple as being above any human consideration. The life of the priest centered on his pre-scribed temple duties at weekly services, such as reading from the Torah, making sacrifices, and preaching. His role at the temple meant more to him than the pain of the man lying at his feet.

This first man was likely on a priestly mission, perhaps on his way to perform his temple duties that very day. No doubt, he remembered the law saying that a man who touched a dead body was unclean for seven days (see Num. 19:11). The priest might have been afraid that the wounded man was dead and refused to risk being made unclean. In his attempt to be holy, he had disconnected himself from the hurting world around him, the wounded whom God loves.

The priest's separation from the world made sense accord-ing to his narrow religious sphere, but it made no sense to the broader world. In the eyes of those outside the Jewish religion, he valued ritual and ceremony more than human life. The priest could only function in his comfort zone, the temple. Outside of that setting, he was like a horse wearing blinders.

The Levite also lived in a reality of his own making, one that was just as false as the priest's. This man saw God's king-dom as a place where the ultimate goal centered around being correct and holding to the right knowledge of God. As a legal expert in Jewish law, the Levite occupied himself with theories and speculations. He perceived power as flowing from doing things right. To him life was an equation, and he was God's answer man. The only problem was, no one outside of his circle was asking the kinds of questions the Levite could answer.

The goal of most churchgoers is to be free from pain, a reality that all of us will experience to one degree or another until the day we die. Old pains are being healed by the Lord's presence and power in our lives, but plenty of new ones keep coming along. We're all trying to forget the personal pain that can either keep us frozen away from the mainstream of the Lord's activity or else open doors into the broader community.

The personal pain of the priest and Levite kept them away from life and focused on their own fears and myths. I'm learning not to allow my pain to keep me paralyzed and sequestered from the world around me that is the object of God's love. Each time I step out of the arena of the church world and into the world of the unchurched, I find that a little bit more of God's healing comes to me.

True Kingdom vision will always be people-centered. The priest and Levite were inwardly centered, caught up in the rules and activities of their religious system. They were in a hurry because they had programs to run. Their programs appeared altogether worthwhile, even biblical and obedient, but these two men were ultimately corrupt because they didn't see people as being at the center of God's kingdom.

INTOLERANCE IS NOT HOLINESS

Scripture required those who served in the temple to be people who lived righteous lives. The priest and Levite no doubt sought personal holiness, a necessary aspiration for all who would follow the Lord. But what these men displayed was not holiness but a counterfeit version that became apparent when they walked past the man lying in the ditch. The priest and Levite were actually seeking to please people rather than God.

When speaking at a church some time ago, I mentioned that sometimes I watch TV and go to the movies. I enjoy going to the movies, I explained, because it is relaxing and serves as a good break from the intensity of my schedule. Later in my talk, I gave an illustration from a popular movie that had been filmed in that state, a movie that Christians would have little difficulty endorsing. When I asked who had seen this film, only two people out of a crowd of over 200 admitted to having done so. The pastor of the church later told me that he personally knew of many members of his congregation who had in fact seen this movie, but they were unwilling to admit it among their friends!

Often what Christians think of as holiness is nothing more than intolerance. This naive approach to following God makes the Christian life seemingly simple: just exclude anyone who violates our image of the Christian life. Worship groups typically set up a code of behavior, rules for following God that take the guesswork out of discipleship. That view of the Christian life allows us to ascertain how we're doing by simply taking an inventory of our outward behavior.

Often what Christians think of as holiness is nothing more than intolerance. This naive approach to following God makes the Christian life seemingly simple: just exclude anyone who violates our image of the Christian life.

One brief set of rules states, "Don't dance, drink, smoke or chew, or go with those girls who do." In theological terms these are called sins of *commission*. The problem with this view of holiness is that we can become oblivious to the primary sin Jesus was addressing in the above parable: sins of *omission*. We do not serve a performance-oriented deity but a God of mercy and forgiveness. Failing to carry out an act of mercy that we know God has placed before us amounts to disobedience and sin.

We can only guess at what the former lives of the priest and Levite were like. Perhaps they had dramatic conversion stories to tell; perhaps they had been raised in their respective traditions from birth. Regardless of their backgrounds, at this point in time they were both clearly out of touch with the world around them. Jesus used the priest and Levite as examples because, to some degree, we all practice the same sort of thinking that prompted them to walk past the wounded man.

While doing a seminar on kindness evangelism in the Kansas City area, we brainstormed about possible ways we could extend God's love into the community. We decided to be a bit different and go after a group that Christians would be unlikely to intersect—New Agers! A gathering of various New Age groups were sponsoring a "psychic fair" at the local convention center. Several hundred of the curious and devoted gathered for the weekend to grow in their knowledge of psychic phenomena.

We stationed ourselves in front of the convention center and gave away free soft drinks. Some members of the evangelism team were a bit fearful of the New Agers. For the most part, they had never spoken to anyone like that but had read enough to be leery. To cope with our own fear and to disarm the conference attendees, we jokingly said, "We're giving away free soft drinks. Don't tell me . . . I'm getting it clearly now. You want a diet Coke, right?!" The people coming into the auditorium were amused and many were open to talking with us further. I count that outreach as especially significant because for the first time I stepped outside of my fears and over a line by speaking with people who believed very differently than I do.

Donald McGavran, a former professor at Fuller Seminary, coined the term "redemption and lift," one that aptly captures the Levite's mentality. While working in India, McGavran noticed a natural improvement in the quality of life of Hindus who came to know Christ. Once these new believers embraced a more biblical lifestyle, their lives became more stable socially, financially and relationally. As followers of Jesus they spent their money differently and tended to live more wisely in general. In short, they began to look more like Christ.

McGavran saw in this trend both a positive side and a negative side. As people were redeemed spiritually and uplifted in their quality of life, they tended to turn away from former relationships with outsiders and live strictly within a new circle of like-minded believers. The redeemed began to feel increasingly uncomfortable relating to their non-Christian friends who held a very different value system. In time they could easily fall prey to a subtle bias that often remains unverbalized: *These poor people around me wouldn't have as much pain in their lives if they were only as wise and together as me.*

Unless we are aware of this phenomenon of redemption and lift, we too will continue to stumble over the next wounded man the Lord lays at our feet. The farther we travel from our personal "B.C." days (Before Christ), the less we remain in touch with the reality of what life apart from Christ is really like. A spiritual arrogance or "sanctified amnesia" can soon settle upon the saints.

The longer we fellowship with other Christians apart from the reality of the world, the more we tend to exaggerate the darkness outside our church walls. We enjoy the Lord so much that we can't remember what it's like to be apart from God. We forget the balanced perspective of the psalmist: "If it had not been the Lord who was on our side" (Ps. 124:1-3). In other words, "There but for the grace of God go I."

WHAT MYTHS KEEP YOU FROM REACHING OUT?

Was the Samaritan always so sensitive to the pain of others? Probably not. It would be unfair to assume that all Samaritans are sensitive or that all Levites and priests are necessarily dull of heart. The difference between these three men was that one had been freed from some stifling myths while the others were still bound by them. After 2,000 years of Church history, many of these same myths likely inhibit you and me from effectively reaching out as well.

What is a myth? Mark Twain said, "In life there are lies and then there are damn lies." In other words, there are blatant lies and subtle lies. A myth is a *subtle lie,* a belief close enough to the truth to be easily confused with pure truth. Myths are doubly dangerous to believers because we easily digest them as truth when we see them modeled by other Christians. When carried out and allowed to influence us over time, they can have a very poisoning effect on our hearts. Here are some religious myths many of us must struggle to overcome.

Myth Number One
My main function in evangelism is to invite nonbelievers to church. Many Christians assume that if we have attractive facilities or well-oiled programs, then people will magically arrive at our doorstep. The people who believe that myth haven't tried to start a church recently. For the most part, the unchurched of our communities really aren't looking for a church to join. In coming to Cincinnati I was told repeatedly, "There are already too many churches in this city." Although their conclusion may be debatable, the *perception* of the average unchurched person is that we already have plenty of churches in America.

Myth Number Two
If a needy person asks me for help, I can excuse myself by apologizing, "Sorry, I don't have the gift of helping." I suspect the Levite thought to himself,

That is not my ministry. I don't rank very high in mercy-giving. I'm more of a teacher. I'd be happy to do a study on the theme of mercy in the minor prophetic books, but I'm not really into the application stuff. Of course, some Christians will be called to more significant ministries of evangelism; a few will even function authentically in the office of evangelist. Paul, however, said that *every* believer is an ambassador for Christ (see 2 Cor. 5:18-20). Jesus sent *us* into the world that the world may believe that God sent Him (see John 17:18-21).

Unfortunately, our attitude toward ministry has been influenced by the specialist mentality that marks our approach to medical services. Dawson Trotman, in his booklet *Born to Reproduce*, makes the excellent point that it is only natural for a healthy human being who is married to another healthy human being to reproduce children. Spiritually reproducing by bringing people into the family of God shouldn't be seen as something unusual at all, but rather as the norm for those who follow Christ.

"Someone really ought to do something about that person in need over there. Of course, that is not my area of responsibility or gifting. I've taken a spiritual gifts test and I scored rather poorly in works of mercy."

When we see a needy person, we too often think (like the priest), *Someone really ought to do something about that person in need over there. Of course, that is not my area of responsibility or gifting. I've taken a spiritual gifts test and I scored rather poorly in works of mercy.* I'm all for people operating according to their greatest gifting, but my own track record tells me that I will regularly be called on to be Jesus to others smack-dab in the middle of my areas of weakness. In fact, God seems to provide training exercises just to help me learn and grow.

For example, our church was attended by many smokers who congregated around the exit doors and then tossed their cigarette butts on the ground. As a nonsmoker, I don't understand that kind of behavior, but I do notice the butts lying around. For many years, I became by default the chief cigarette-butt-picker-upper. At first I wondered how "those insensitive smokers" could possibly not notice what they were doing. Now I believe that those butts are part of God's work of attitude-adjustment in my own life.

Myth Number Three

This person doesn't look like a good candidate for conversion. Upon hearing the basic idea of servant evangelism, one pastor responded with alarm, "What you're saying could be dangerous. I could see this thing getting out of hand. Before you know it the world would just be coming into the church. It seems things would get out of control pretty quickly." I responded, "I don't mean to be disrespectful, but what you're describing is exactly the goal. My intention is to see that things do get out of hand. There is something refreshing about having more going on than one person can control."

The word "careful" implies that matters are in our hands instead of the Lord's. When the responsibility for a situation is resting upon our strength or capabilities, we will inevitably become "full of care" for the outcome. It is not my call or anyone else's to author or maintain the life of God in others. We can function as God's representatives but we cannot bear the responsibility for His people. God alone can "bring to completion" the good work that He has started (Phil. 1:6). And I believe that what God has begun, He will maintain.

Evangelism Samaritan-Style

Jesus makes the Samaritan the hero of this parable—something that must have shocked the Jews listening to Him. As the brunt of jokes in that day, Samaritans were stereotyped as simple, rural people who were slow and uneducated. However, Jesus applauded this man's attitudes and actions as reflecting an accurate view of God's kingdom as a *merciful kingdom*. We learn from the Samaritan's example that when we step out to touch the lost, God's presence meets us and equips us to bring healing. In other words, the kingdom of God flows through those who are open to being dispensers of God's love and presence.

Jesus captures this thought when He quotes from Isaiah 61: "The Spirit of the Lord is upon me, because he has anointed me to preach . . . to heal . . . to set at liberty . . . to proclaim" (Luke 4:18-19). We see that the inflow of the Lord's anointing is intricately tied to the outflow of our efforts to help others experience more of God's mercy. In fact, I have found that His presence and life are never more present than when I am giving away God's love to those who are hurting and lost. As we bring the message of God's mercy to the lost and needy, His anointing will be upon us as well to meet their needs.

The parable of the lost sheep (see Luke 15:3-7) makes it clear that God highly values those who are not yet gathered into His fold. Scripture tells us that He rejoices more over the one who is lost and then found than over the ninety-nine already safe and sound. Jesus modeled to us the outflowing of His kingdom wherever He went. He came to seek and to heal the lost—which included the sick lost, the imprisoned lost, the lame lost, or the poor lost. The Good Shepherd actively sought out unbelievers. In fact, He spent the better part of His ministry with those outside of established religion. And whenever Jesus was with the lost, He sensed the Father's very personal love for them and His desire to draw them into His kingdom.

In the same way, the Samaritan was anointed with God's grace when he stopped to help this wounded man. As he stepped out to show mercy to a stranger, he was loving the people whom

God is especially committed to. The priest and Levite experienced no such anointing because they didn't step out to give
aid. My guess is that they hesitated to help because they didn't
feel equipped or inspired. Maybe they were just tired. However,
had the priest and Levite taken the time to extend a helping
hand, they would have found ample amounts of God's favor to
meet their needs.

GETTING BEYOND OURSELVES

No matter how long we may have been stuck in wrong attitudes or approaches to the unchurched, we can still change.
What practices can we build into our lives that would help us
to share God's love more effectively? The following principles
can be learned by reflecting on the actions of the priest, Levite
and Samaritan.

Be "With the People"

If you long for more of God's heart, you'll probably get it simply
by spending time with the unchurched. This phrase "with the
people" is repeated often in the book of Acts. Leaders of the Early
Church were continually with the people, both inside and outside the fold of God. They lived out the opposite lifestyle from
the priest and Levite, who believed that the secret to success
meant being separated from the people. They believed that one
could hear God more accurately by getting away from people.

The old preacher's adage seems true: "Either we will obey
Acts 1:8, or we will experience Acts 8:1." In the first text, Jesus
calls us to be His witnesses beginning in Jerusalem and on to
Judea, Samaria, and ultimately to the ends of the earth. Acts 8:1
tells us that "on that day a great persecution arose against the
church in Jerusalem; and they were all scattered throughout the
region of Judea and Samaria."

Jesus sent His followers to sow the seeds of God's love to the ends of the earth, to dispel the grip of darkness by proclaiming the gospel. After some years it became obvious that most people were satisfied with sowing seeds in the same locale. No one wanted to leave Jerusalem and go to the ends of the earth. Consequently the local church had seeds piled up waist deep and going to waste. As South American evangelist Luis Palau says, Christians are a lot like fertilizer. Piled up in one place they will burn a hole in the ground beneath them. But spread out over a large field, they can do a lot of good!

One way or another, the Lord is intent on getting the Church out of its own little circle and out into the presence of the world He loves. God is serious about wanting to reach the unleavened parts of our world with the good news of Jesus Christ.

Christians are a lot like fertilizer. Piled up in one place they will burn a hole in the ground beneath them. But spread out over a large field, they can do a lot of good!

Step Out of Your Comfort Zone

In order to have any impact on the life of the wounded stranger, the Samaritan had to step out in faith. The Samaritan didn't seek to separate himself as the priest or Levite had. Rather, like Christ, he entered into the heart of the world and got involved in its pain face to face.

The Samaritan's actions reflect Jesus' image of the kingdom of God as comparable to a mustard seed: "It is like a mustard seed which, when it is sown on the ground, is smaller than all the seeds on earth; but when it is sown, it grows up, becomes greater than all herbs, and shoots out large branches, so that the birds of the air may nest under its shade" (Mark 4:31-32).

Christians tend to congregate. We are naturally drawn to community where we sense the strong presence of God. Community is part of what we are to be about, but a community of light without outward focus can quickly turn into a burned-out community. The purpose of light is defeated unless it penetrates the darkness. The nature of God within every believer is in direct conflict with any tendency we may have to hold onto the presence of God like a miser clutching gold.

Bring the Kingdom

The Samaritan *brought* the kingdom of God as the answer to the wounded man's needs. He saw the kingdom of God as vital and living, reaching the pain of the lost and touching them directly. Jesus didn't *send* the truth and life of God; He *became* the truth and life. He entered the plane of humanity to show us what human life could be like when it was centered on God's love. Jesus didn't send the love of God; He brought that love to those who were in need.

My hunch is that the Samaritan suffered some immediate accusations because of his involvement with the wounded man. We too will sometimes be misunderstood as we step out to share God's love. For some time, I went to a local abortion clinic and demonstrated God's love to those on both sides of the abortion issue. I am definitely against abortion, but I felt that the best way to soften hard hearts was to enter the situation with the power of kindness. I have given out free coffee and soft drinks and washed the windshields of everyone there.

The pro-abortion people thought I was a little weird. They may have thought, *We know he's up to something; we just haven't figured it out yet.* The Christians, on the other hand, were often less than graceful toward me. I often heard catcalls such as, "Next time bring your anti-abortion sign with you." The anti-abortion activists saw no point in what we were doing and suspected our stance on abortion as being soft.

Mother Teresa dealt with misunderstanding like this for years. She captured a wonderful balance when she described the mission of the Sisters of Charity: "We are contemplatives that live in the heart of the world twenty-four hours a day." The Samaritan exhibited this same balance and Jesus identified him as a hero.

Begin to Care

It sounds simple, but we can decide to open our hearts and begin to care. We can decide to allow our hearts to become sensitive again to the pain of others. God has shaped our hearts to notice the needs that grieve Him. Wherever our hearts have become hardened over the years, they can become softened and pliable again. Begin with a simple prayer. Ask God to give you His heart, to help you see the way He sees.

It is one thing to see and quite another to notice. The priest and Levite *saw* the beaten man with their eyes, but they really didn't *notice*. The Samaritan's heart was sensitive to noticing the pain of others. We would be mistaken to think that the Good Samaritan was going through life just looking for someone to help. He was apparently a businessman, someone used to schedules and appointments. He was probably on a business trip, traveling an established trade route, one known to the bandits as well. He may have passed that way on many other occasions, as evidenced by the reaction of the innkeeper. I'm sure that he had important affairs on his mind, but he put them aside because he cared about this stranger in need.

Make Yourself Available

Begin in prayer, and then look for those God will send your way. The Lord is looking for people who want to be used by Him to carry His mercy to the world. He hears the cry of our hearts whenever we pray, but God seems especially receptive to prayers of availability. I have challenged many people over the years to begin their trek toward greater usefulness by asking God to send them opportunities. I have seldom met someone who didn't see immediate and encouraging answers to that sort of prayer.

While I was doing a seminar in Baton Rouge, a pastor confided in me that he had been stuck inside the four walls of the church for some years. Excited about this idea of kindness evangelism, he wondered if he could break out of his personal safety zone. After participating in a large soft-drink outreach at an LSU football game, this man came back very enthused at what he'd seen. His group of 25 had given away more than 600 drinks to those driving into the stadium parking lot.

During lunch this pastor confessed to me that he had spent most of his Christian life maintaining the same fears he had as a non-Christian. In particular he had harbored a fear of the black community. He couldn't offer a rational explanation, but for years he had held a disdain for the blacks of his city. That day, as he gave away soft drinks, something broke in him. The last I talked to this pastor, he told me he had built a shoeshine kit and regularly visited a local grocery market on Saturday mornings to offer free shoeshines. Many of his customers were black men. As he made himself available, the fears that had kept him captive for years dissipated.

Many of us started out our Christian walk with an attitude of availability, an approach to life that said, "Whatever, Lord." Convinced that God's power could change any human heart, we were willing to risk all to be obedient to Christ. Then somewhere along the way, we lost this gambler's attitude. Disappointments, unrealistic expectations, and the trauma of life slowly took the wind from our sails. Perhaps our enthusiasm was dented by watching other believers with what we considered to be a far less available and obedient attitude.

Many of us started out our Christian walk
with an attitude of availability that said,
"Whatever, Lord"... Then somewhere along the
way, we lost this gambler's attitude.

Now is the time to return to our first love for Christ. For me the key has been to realize that if I wait until all of my questions are answered and all of my problems are healed, then I will never get launched into ministry to the lost. I must be willing to live with some tension between my current lack and God's promise of provision.

Manage Your Fear by Going with a Group

I go out to do kindness evangelism at least once per week. Having maintained this schedule for many years now, I am still a bit fearful every time I go out. My hunch is that we will never be completely free from our fears. They are simply part of the human predicament. In order to overcome them, we must find fellowship in our fears. Whenever we went out to do ministry, I told my people, "We can be afraid together and go out into the community."

Most of the people I speak to about doing kindness evangelism don't realize that I'm fearful most of the time when going out to do ministry. I score as an introvert on personality inventories. I also have a low need for adventure. The ideal workday for me is being in an office alone working uninterruptedly on projects. Recognizing that I will always have to deal with my fear to some extent, I will be wiser to seek to *manage* my fears of interacting with unbelievers. I became more effective as a leader when I stopped looking for fear*less* people and just began to work with others who are willing to manage their fears along with me. The key is being in a group where we can more readily sense God's presence. Also, courage is contagious.

I was in Queens, New York, teaching for several days at New Life Fellowship. After talking about evangelism each morning, we went out into the community for several hours of hands-on practice. We experimented with several servant evangelism projects to get an idea of what would work in this section of the Big Apple. One rather large team enthusiastically took on a free car wash. Remarkably, in four hours they washed 250 cars.

A skeptical taxi driver slowed down and yelled out, "Why in the *@*! are you fooling people? That's not very &%#! nice for you Christians to lie to people by telling them you're washing cars free when you're really not." One man holding a sign announcing the car wash responded back, "It really is free. We really mean it. No donations accepted. We're doing this just to show you that God loves you incredibly." The man was incredulous and drove on.

Two minutes later he came back, rolled his window down, and asked, "Is this *really* free?" After one more assurance, he pulled in and let us wash his car, even though he was still a little skeptical. A few moments later the pace of cars pulling in picked up and even those carrying the signs went to work washing. The skeptical taxi driver volunteered to hold one of the "Free Car Wash—No Kidding" signs. In true New York taxi-driver fashion, he was yelling as people drove by, "Hey you, get in here! It really is free! I didn't believe them either, but they really are doing this just to show you God's love!" Out of the mouths of babes . . . or hardened taxi drivers.

Realize That Failure Is a Given

I believe the priest in Jesus' story was profoundly fearful of failure. "I might step out to do something and fall flat on my face."

That is a realistic fear. My encouragement to you is that you *will* fall flat on your face. Failure is predictable! Realizing that fact gives me a lot of courage.

A message I frequently repeated to our leaders and workers was this: "Isn't it wonderful that we can obey the call to do evangelism realizing that failure is just around the corner? The only unknown in our outreach is *how* we're going to fail and exactly *when* we're going to fail." We took as our motto a saying of George Bernard Shaw: "Anything worth doing is worth doing wrong." Ours was not to demand success but to see every opportunity as a learning experience that would mold us into more capable servants for Christ.

I sometimes feel like Dorothy and her friends in *The Wizard of Oz*. As they continued on their journey, they began to focus on everything that might go wrong and began to chant, "Lions, tigers, and bears, oh my!" Not one vicious lion, tiger or bear ever appeared during the whole trip. As in that movie, most of our fears never materialize.

This timeless story taps into our experiences of entering into the world: It is a scary and overwhelming place, especially at first. As with Dorothy, few of our fears are as bad as we first think. When she finally encountered the enemy face to face, Dorothy discovered that the wicked witch was not so powerful after all. Just a little water finished her off.

In my years of going out into the community, I have discovered that the *fear* of failure is much worse than failure itself. A recent survey asked several hundred American men to name their number one fear. I was surprised to learn the results. I thought that fear of death would be at the top, but it came in fourth. The fear of growing bald was even further down the list. The number one anxiety of American men was the fear of losing their jobs.

A follow-up survey six months later queried the men who had actually lost their jobs. Consistently, the respondents indicated that *losing their jobs* was one of the most positive things that had ever happened to them. Many discovered new careers they had long dreamed about but had been fearful of venturing into as long as they were employed. When we turn and face our fears, we discover that the dread of loss is truly stronger than the loss itself.

Sow Liberally

In ancient times, sowing seed was done very differently than it is today. Modern farmers first plow to break up the hard soil and *then* sow the seed. In Jesus' day, seed was thrown and then the soil was plowed. Wherever seed was flung, there would be action of some sort later on.

When we plant a seed of love, we can be assured that some of God's presence will be deposited. At some point in time, depending on many variables, that seed will hopefully grow to produce a plant. The fact that some soil was rocky, full of weeds, or shallow did not preclude its receiving seed and producing some growth. The best soil and the right conditions of light, soil and weeding produced the most growth, but the farmer in Jesus' parable did not limit his sowing to good soil alone.

When I was 10, my brother and I planted a backyard garden at our home in Wichita, Kansas. Our mom let us plant our sections of the garden however we wanted. I carefully read the directions on the back of the seed packet and even looked in an encyclopedia to find out how carrots should be planted. My rows were straight, orderly, parallel—just like the instructions said they should be. In fact, I did everything right . . . except for one detail: I planted my seeds too deep in the soil.

Erik was four at the time and had a very different approach to planting than I did. He took the entire contents of his two seed packets and threw them on the ground over a one-square-foot diameter. After several weeks we had two very different gardens. Erik had dozens of pencil-sized carrots in his, while I had nothing to show for my careful, hard work. I discovered later that I had planted my carrots about an inch too deep. My brother had hardly planted his seeds, but because they were fertile they basically rooted themselves in the good soil. Erik's approach wasn't pretty, but it did produce an abundance of carrots.

We need to be a little more like Erik in our approach to evangelism. The most important lesson that we can draw from the story of the sower is that God's presence follows the seeds that are planted and bestows power and blessing on the seed apart from the sower. The key is understanding that life is in the seed itself. The sower's role was to fling the seed—hopefully on good ground. With an abundance of seed available, he was unconcerned about the results.

Our job is to be seed flingers, not seed protectors watching over God's business as though He had a limited supply.

Jesus called all who would hear Him to come into the family of God. He came "to seek and to save that which was lost" (Luke 19:10). To "seek" means to "invite in." We can assume that God is actively drawing everyone to Himself, whether or not they look like they're responding. There are no categories of people, some that He's calling and some He's not. God's desire is to include the entire human race in His family, even the most unlikeable villains on the planet. "The Lord is . . . not willing that any should perish but that all should come to repentance" (2 Pet. 3:9). Not everyone will respond to His invitation, but God's attitude remains the same.

In the Clint Eastwood Western *Unforgiven*, the main character had a couple of gun-slinging allies. They were all major tough guys, of course, but one of them had a humorous twist: He was incredibly nearsighted and couldn't shoot straight. The remedy? Shoot in all directions, reload and continue shooting. He figured that he was bound to hit something eventually if he just kept at it. The attitude of this shooter is similar to the approach of the sower in the parable. God has no shortage of bullets or seed. We have tended to underestimate his resources and have proceeded more like Barney Fife on the *Andy Griffith Show*—as though we had just one bullet! We can let loose and shoot in all directions because we have an infinite supply of ammunition.

Our job is to be seed flingers, not seed protectors watching over God's business as though He had a limited supply. If we are sowing the seed of God's kingdom, there will be no shortage of seed. As soon as we sow what we have, there is more in its place. The value for sowing liberally is captured in Ecclesiastes 11:1-2: "Cast your bread upon the waters, for you will find it after many days. Give a serving to seven, and also to eight, for you do not know what evil will be on the earth." We cast the bread and God causes the results.

When I began to do evangelism, I saw myself as a sower to whom God had granted a small amount of seed to sow. Assuming I had only a thimbleful of seed to last me a lifetime, I would be foolish to plant any except in the most fertile places. Consequently, I sowed God's love carefully and sparingly—much as I had my small garden plot in Kansas. I came to realize that deeds of love are meant to be sown in a broadcast fashion, as modeled by the sower in Jesus' parable.

SOWING EVERYWHERE, EVEN PINKIE'S BAR

Every Saturday morning at 10:00 is a special time at our church—the time when groups go out into the community to serve in

practical ways. Some take food and clothing to the poor; others
do various servant evangelism projects. One Saturday I was
with a team that was washing the windows of businesses in
downtown Cincinnati, including retail stores, restaurants and
even an occasional bar.

On this particular Saturday, my last stop was Pinkie's Bar.
It was about noon and the place was full of customers, with
Waylon Jennings "wayling" on the corner jukebox. This was no
classy place—beer was served in the can. I asked the woman
tending bar if I could wash their front windows as a simple
expression of God's love. With little reaction she said, "Whatever
turns you on."

As I began to clean the windows with a teammate, a group of
four customers called me over to the bar. "We heard what you
said to the bartender about doing this to show God's love. We
want to know what kind of church would do something like this."

I spent several minutes telling them about our fellowship.
Then a woman with tears brimming in her eyes asked, "Do you
think people like us would fit into a church like yours?"

Recalling this story serves as a wonderful progress check for
me. Several years ago I probably would have instantly answered,
"Yes, of course!" But the disdain in my voice would have caused
her to question whether she was really invited. My heart would
have said, "We're Christians. Don't you know that's what Christians do? We love people!" If she had come, however, she would
have met people who wouldn't have necessarily welcomed her
into their hearts. She would have encountered people influenced by the myths and fears we've discussed in this chapter.
My own false perceptions about non-Christians had convinced
me at one point that only the lowest forms of life on the planet
hang around bars.

God has since shown me a different kind of love, a fertile
love that reaches out toward everyone. For years I loved the lost

in obedience to God and His Word. In recent years something has shifted in my heart. I feel I've grown. Now I don't just love the lost; I even like them.

More Kindness

How are you doing on the "us and them" thing? Maybe you need to do what I do when I feel that insidious mentality coming on: I go clean a toilet!

Oh, so you aren't a porcelain prince or princess? Okay, how about this: Head for the nearest coffee store—not the 7-Eleven—and get in a nice long line. When you've ordered your venti frappi-mocha-shappalino, turn to the person behind you and say with a big smile, "What are you having today?" When he or she tells you, say to the cashier, "Add his/her coffee to my order, please."

When the inevitable questions and protests arise, just say, "I wanted to show you God's love in a practical way." If your church has a connect card, give them one. If your church doesn't have a connect card, go to conspiracyofkindness.com and we will send you a kindness package that includes one—no strings attached.

Five Discoveries
That Empower Evangelism

When strangers start acting like neighbors . . .
communities are reinvigorated.
RALPH NADER

If there is any kindness I can show, or any good thing I can do
to any fellow being, let me do it now, and not deter or neglect it,
as I shall not pass this way again.
WILLIAM PENN

I took my first stab at premeditated kindness by organizing a free car wash while my wife, Janie, and I were starting a church in Oslo, Norway. The first customer's bumper sticker identified the driver as a member of the Socialist Agnostic political party. Our Norwegian friends felt utterly incapable of talking to this woman for fear she would come at them with mind-boggling arguments they'd be unable to answer.

The worst fear of all Scandinavians was being realized: the possibility of looking bad in public. It had taken me six weeks to convince this small group that an outreach would be "big fun" and now they were not having one bit of fun. Even though I spoke Norwegian with a noticeable accent, I engaged our customer in conversation. "Hi, we're going to wash your car for free and we're not going to allow you to give us any money for this."

"Okay, but why?"

"We want to show you God's love in a tangible way. His love is free and so is ours!" I said.

By the time we finished washing her car, to the amazement of the Norwegian Christians, this lady was weeping. She was experiencing reverse sticker shock—we *wouldn't* take her money. She rolled down the window and said, "I am 50 years old and have lived in a so-called Christian nation all my life. I've heard people talk and talk and talk about God for a long time and have opposed them. I determined a long time ago they weren't real in their love, so He must not be real. But today, this is the first time I have *experienced* any of God's love. What I have seen here is real!"

"I am 50 years old and have lived in a so-called Christian nation all my life. I've heard people talk and talk and talk about God for a long time and have opposed them. . . . But today, this is the first time I have experienced any of God's love."

As she pulled away, two Mormon missionaries drove up. Their clip-on black ties, little black name tags, white shirts, and distinctive short haircuts gave them away from a distance. As we washed their car, these young missionaries from Utah were also surprised we wouldn't take their money.

"So, why are you doing this?" they asked.

"Just to show you God's love in a practical way." I had never met a speechless Mormon missionary. All those I had met over the years were not one bit shy about giving their memorized speech, but we had two dumbfounded Mormon missionaries standing before us. They had nothing to say because we had beaten them to the punch with a demonstration of the reality of God that no verbal comeback could match.

Janie and I learned many valuable lessons from that year in Norway. We learned about enduring in the midst of difficulty, keeping on with a project even without much response, and doing what we do as unto the Lord and not to people. St. John of the Cross, in his book *Dark Night of the Soul*, explains how God allows all of us to go through trauma and testing in order to bring us to new levels of dependence upon Him.[1] God even allows us to feel abandoned by Him and others so that we will grow in faithfulness, regardless of our emotions. This author suggests that all of us go through those "dark nights" occasionally because we don't grow spiritually except in times of adversity.

Our dark night of the soul occurred during our year in Norway. True to the prediction of St. John of the Cross, we emerged from this time of isolation with important spiritual and emotional growth under our belts. We had to develop a never-say-die attitude in Norway because the people there were not looking for what we had to offer. We arrived in Cincinnati in 1983 thinking it would be different. We were wrong.

THE HOWARD BEALE EXPERIENCE

Cincinnati is friendly, but in a skeptical kind of way. New ideas don't catch on quickly there. I noticed when we first moved to the city that Cincinnatians wear belts and suspenders at the same time, clear evidence of conservatism. Mark Twain wrote more than 100 years ago, "When the end of time comes, I want to be in Cincinnati because everything happens 10 years later there."

Not only was the weather cold, damp and unwelcoming to two former Californians, but we also found the people skeptical of the new ideas we presented. Our new fellowship grew at a snail's pace. From my early Christian days as part of the Jesus

Movement, I was conditioned to think that my job was to open the Bible and automatically large crowds would assemble. I was wrong.

I felt a lot like Howard Beale, a main character in the movie titled *Network*. This veteran newsman is unexpectedly given the option to retire or be fired to make room for a more youthful replacement. Instead of offering the expected niceties in his last editorial comment on the air, Beale begins to talk from his heart. He voices frustration over his sense of ineffectiveness in life and confesses that he has been ruled by his fears.

As his career comes to a close, Howard Beale expresses remorse that he spent his life playing roles and knuckling under to everyone's expectations around him. Now, on his last day at work, he decides to express the depths of his heart. His swan song concludes with the exhortation, "Wherever you are, I want you to get up, go to your window, open it and yell as loudly as you can, 'I'm mad as hell and I'm *not* going to take it anymore!'" Seemingly all of New York City promptly joins in with this one man's chorus of rebellion.

Howard Beale was stuck on a skip in the record that seemed to play over and over, "Play out your expected role." He never explored or discovered who he really was. That approach to life can only be lived out so long, until one comes to a crisis or something inside of us dies. Beale finally decided to reveal his heart and convictions without caring whether or not the critics around him approved.

I found myself at that same point in my own life. I was tired of being careful about starting this new church and making sure it was done the "right" way. I was frustrated at my own sense of ineffectiveness, at my unwillingness to take the risky route to evangelism that Jesus seemed to always take. For most of my Christian life, the message had played loud and clear, "Play the expected role."

I had been stuck in a mode of perpetual preparation—continually getting ready for the work of God's kingdom, acquiring equipment for spiritual warfare that would never be used unless I got outside the castle walls. As a leader I was very focused on the idea of getting the people properly prepared. My life's motto could have been phrased, "Ready, aim . . . Ready, aim . . . Ready, aim . . ." I was stuck in a state of perpetual readiness. I never got to "fire."

"Fire" meant stepping out to change. Like many Christians, I was fearful of obeying the Lord—afraid of change, afraid of failure, afraid of disappointment if things didn't go well. I would have never admitted to resisting the forward progress of God's kingdom, but my fearful attitude toward change served as a continual blockage. My vision was so small and narrow it made me and what I was doing seem boring and unattractive to outsiders. As low as our numbers were, I was still fearful of losing the little that we had accumulated.

> *My life's motto could have been phrased,*
> *"Ready, aim . . . Ready, aim . . . Ready,*
> *aim . . ." I was stuck in a state of perpetual*
> *readiness. I never got to "fire."*

The changing point for me came while sitting at a restaurant one day. I had just shared my vision for starting this new church—and had been rejected once again—when I felt the Lord speak to me. He said volumes in just a short space: *"If you will befriend My friends, I will send you more people than you will know what to do with."*

I had no idea who God's "friends" were, but those words proved to be a turning point in my heart and in our fledgling church. Sheer desperation pushed me to see the Christian life and evangelism in new ways. Over the next several weeks, I searched the Scriptures, prayed and asked, "Who are God's friends?" I began to see a trend in the New Testament texts that I hadn't noticed before. Although Jesus loved everybody, He apparently *enjoyed* some people more than others. His heart especially went out to the poor, the sick and the lost. Even the 12 men Jesus chose as His disciples (with the exception of Judas Iscariot) were from Galilee, the poor section of Palestine.

I knew that my job was to minister to the hurting, but I didn't know how. I had done plenty of door knocking and knew it didn't work for me. Besides, people were more skeptical of the Church than ever. After all, hadn't I already received several hundred rejections to my invitation of being involved in this new fellowship?

Then a new idea began to form. If I could somehow relieve an ounce of the pain that someone was going through, maybe then we could get that person's attention. If our church could meet people on the basis of serving our way into their hearts, maybe then we would have an audience. Servant evangelism was born out of this realization that as we touch people at their point of pain—whether the need was for food, healing or wisdom—they would open the door of their hearts and invite us into their lives.

I had come to Cincinnati with the wrong goal. My ambition of starting a new church was much too narrow. The goal that was worth pursuing was much more central to the heart of God: to bring the kingdom of God to this city through acts of love and mercy. Everything in the Christian life flows out of the first commandment: to love God with our heart, soul, strength and mind. That *vertical love*, from God to us, lays the foundation for any other love. *Horizontal love* for our neighbor overflows out of the love of God.

Once I believed in a goal that was worth accomplishing, I was beginning to have God's heart. Consequently, my internal orders started to change. The new assignment was to find ways to relieve people's pain. But how could I encounter these people? How could I overcome their skepticism, their tendency to misinterpret any attempts to reach out to them? Let me share with you five discoveries that empowered me to bring Christ to others.

1. PEOPLE LISTENED WHEN I TREATED THEM LIKE FRIENDS

Even though we saw the power of kindness in our first attempt at servant evangelism in Oslo, the results were scarce. That same project in Cincinnati bore fruit immediately. We displayed several banners reading "ABSOLUTELY FREE CAR WASH—NO MONEY ACCEPTED." A couple of former cheerleaders stood on the corner with signs directing dirty cars to our crew. The rest of the team waited to begin washing, cleaning windows and tires, and vacuuming. We also had a couple of designated talkers to share *why* we were doing this. Lots of people drove by with a jaded look on their face as if to say, "Right. I'm sure this is free. Nothing is really for free. There's got to be a catch."

Our first customer was a haggard-looking, single mom with a half dozen squirming kids in an old station wagon. We could see in her eyes that life had been hard on her. We gave her a cold drink and explained our project while her car was washed from top to bottom. Before leaving, she asked for prayer and cried a little as we asked God to begin to show Himself to her. This mother left with a smile on her face. It was clear that our small gift of service had turned her day around.

The second car that pulled in was a stainless steel Delorean sports car whose gray-haired driver was a well-known wealthy Cincinnatian. "How much?" he asked.

"It's free," we answered. The man nodded slightly with a quizzical look.

As we finished, he asked, "To whom shall I make out my check?"

"No, sir," someone told him again, "we really aren't taking any money for washing your car. We did this just because God loves you." He repeated himself and began to show some signs of irritation that we were so slow in understanding his simple question. For the third time, I told him we wouldn't take his money because this really was a *free* car wash. To my surprise tears welled up in his eyes. In a world full of the "work hard and then you are rewarded" approach to life, our free gift seemed beyond reason. This man seemed very touched.

Many other people were strongly touched that afternoon in a way mere talk couldn't accomplish. We closed our time in prayer and shed a few tears of gratefulness for God's favor. After three hours we had washed over 40 cars. Someone commented to me, "Jesus was right. It really is more blessed to give than receive." That day we began to see and feel the pain of those we served. We sensed our hearts being enlarged and looking more like His than when we'd begun. Most important, we had made a lasting discovery: People respond to the message of the church when we approach them as friends.

Excluders or Includers

German sociologist Ferdinand Tonnies authored a famous book in the 1800s called *Gemeinschaft und Gesellschaft*. In this study, the author identified small communities as being built on one-to-one relationships and the exclusive sense of a small family as *gemeinschaft*. On the other hand, the *gesellschaft* approach to relationships operates on the basis of inclusion.

The first sort of relationships are cozy but exclusive. Gemeinschaft groups typically appear to be friendly, but they quickly deny access to newcomers who are different. The thinking here is, *I cannot associate with you unless you become like me. You must leave your circle and join mine, for I am unwilling to change.* These primary groups are nearly impossible to invade unless newcomers are capable of adapting to their established social standards.

One of the most common ways Christians exclude outsiders is through our language. Newcomers catch on very quickly as to whether our fellowships are open or closed by what kind of jargon we use. The following extreme renditions of some simple sayings may give you some idea as to how outsiders may feel when they listen to us:

- *Dead men tell no tales:* "Male cadavers are incapable of yielding any testimony."
- *Cleanliness is next to godliness:* "Freedom from encrustations of grime is contiguous to rectitude."
- *Look before you leap:* "Surveillance should precede saltation."
- *Twinkle, twinkle, little star:* "Scintillate, scintillate, asteroid minifid."
- *He who laughs last, laughs best:* "Abstention from presenting the ultimate cachination possesses thereby the optimal cachination."

While the *gemeinschaft* approach shrinks the opening to a group, the *gesellschaft* approach creates a funnel that makes it easy for an individual to gain entry. It's as if all of us have a funnel of some size resting over our heads, with the size of the opening determined by the size of our hearts. If we are seeking to be includers like Jesus, we will experience ever-growing funnels that are receptive to new people and new ideas. If we live as excluders, our shrinking funnels will keep out more than we allow into our lives.

Jesus says, "Whoever comes to me I will never drive away" (John 6:37). "Whoever" meant that all were welcome to be His friends. His funnel was large enough to encompass us all. Throughout His life, Jesus made a habit of hanging around with unpopular people like prostitutes, outlaws, the poor, the diseased, the demonized—not the crowd most of us spend time with every day. Yet they were open to Jesus and to His message. That's what counted. Because they were open to being loved by Him, God extended His love to them.

Since Jesus' love and acceptance includes everyone, we all need to be constantly striving to increase the capacity of our hearts. To the degree that we love and accept people the way they are, without preconditions or culturally prescribed expectations, to that degree we love the way God loves. Our hearts are never static; they are either growing or shrinking. The benchmark of an expanding heart is one that is *unoffendable* by those who are different. To keep our hearts growing, we must walk in the *agape* or unconditional love Jesus showed us in the miracles He performed, and ultimately, demonstrated on the cross.

2. WHEN I SERVE, HEARTS ARE TOUCHED

One evening in the mid-sixties, I was out in the car with my dad having a father and son talk—something we usually did the day report cards came out. I was no honor roll student then, but this was a particularly poor grading period for me. Trying to be constructive in his criticism, my dad referred to the attendant at the gas station as an example. "Steve, you've got to do better with your grades if you expect to get anywhere in life. If you don't start doing better," Dad said, pointing to the man washing the windshield, "you're going to end up washing windshields and cleaning toilets for a living when you grow up." As it turns out, he was a prophet and didn't know it!

My dad's image of people who serve in menial ways is pretty common, typified by Goober on the *Andy Griffith Show*. Goober manned the gas pumps at the local gas station, checked oil levels, and washed windshields. A man who took pleasure in the simple things in life, Goober was negatively portrayed as a simple-minded guy with little hope for a better future. Our culture often paints such a picture of people who serve—as slow, uneducated people who couldn't make anything of themselves and ended up taking whatever work they could find. We might speak disdainfully of someone, saying, "Cousin Bob works with his hands," meaning he couldn't get any other work.

"Steve, if you don't start getting better grades,"
Dad said, pointing to the man washing the
windshield, "you're going to end up washing
windshields and cleaning toilets for a living
when you grow up." As it turns out, he was
a prophet and didn't know it!

That attitude may represent the thinking of the world system, but it is the opposite of the scriptural model. As Christians, it is our nature to serve. We are indwelled by the Holy Spirit, that same Spirit who lived through Jesus while He walked the earth. Paul concisely describes Jesus' life and ministry in terms of a servant: "Let this mind be in you which was also in Christ Jesus, who, being in the form of God, did not consider it robbery to be equal with God, but made himself of no reputation, taking the form of a servant, and coming in the likeness of men. And being found in appearance as a man, he humbled himself and became obedient to the point of death, even the death of the cross" (Phil. 2:5-8).

When we come to Christ, God grants us a new nature that is entirely different from our old self-centered one that sought to be served. As we encounter the life of God, we come to have the same nature as that of Jesus Christ. As we live out that nature by serving others, we are able to influence the lives of others.

The call of God is in direct opposition to our cultural conditioning. I was raised in an upper-middle-class, ethnic home that valued hard work. The unspoken motto of my Scandinavian relatives was, "You get what you work for." I grew to see the poor, the sick and the lost as people who were getting what they had worked for—and what they deserved. My oversimplified view of life told me that my family did well because we were wise and hardworking.

John 13 records the events of the Last Supper, a clear example of the priority Jesus placed on serving. Gayle Erwin explores the significance of this meeting in his book *The Jesus Style*:

> Imagine Jesus, biceps bulging beneath a seamless robe with flowing cape, reclining at supper with his disciples. The forces of evil have been collecting for months and are about to kill him, but don't worry, all the power ever created is coursing through his body. He gets up—this man surrounded by overwhelming evil forces—walks over to the disciples, and with all this incredible power . . . begins to do what? "He got up from the meal, took off his outer clothing, and wrapped a towel around his waist. After that, he poured water into a basin and began to wash his disciples' feet. . . ." So that is what He does with power—He washes feet![2]

We can choose to do battle in two different arenas. We can either try to convince others in the arena of the *mind* or we can approach people in the arena of the *heart*. For the most part, traditional approaches to evangelism go head to head instead of heart to heart. We assume that if we could just get unbelievers to *think* straight, then we would see them come to Christ. Having equated salvation with a mental assent to particular doctrines, we try to enter peoples' lives by way of argumentation.

The mind certainly plays a part in coming to Christ, but the will is central in what Scripture frequently refers to as the heart. *The Evangelical Dictionary of Theology* defines "heart" in the biblical sense as meaning "the center or focus of man's personal life, the spring of all his desires, motives, and moral choices—indeed, of all his behavioral trends." Thus, when we touch the heart, we have touched a person at the deepest level.

The exciting news is that the heart isn't unreachable. Our experience has shown that a person's heart is most quickly touched by acts of service. A Norwegian expression wonderfully captures this idea: *"kjokken veien"* or "the kitchen way in." In other words, coming in the back door, the pleasant, easy door. This kitchen-door entrance with the gospel revolves around acts of practical service. In other words, we truly enter the lives of others in evangelism when we touch their hearts.

Although we may use other entry points—perhaps appealing to people's minds or emotions—ultimately we must, according to Scripture, invade their hearts. And the sooner we get to the heart of those we are seeking to lead to Jesus, the better able we are to connect with them at their core. Servant evangelism enables us to quickly touch the heart—the decision-making center of a person's life—and make a lasting impact. If the human heart is the ultimate target of our evangelism, why not shoot for the heart from the first moment of our encounter with non-Christians?

3. As I Serve, I Redefine the Perception of a Christian

A small-group leader from a church in eastern Canada told me about his experience in front of a local donut shop. His group was washing windshields in the parking lot when they noticed several customers watching them. After some discussion inside the shop, a sharply dressed businessman came out. With a British accent he said, "We've been watching you from inside the shop washing our windshields and were just wondering why you're doing this."

The leader answered, "We're showing God's love to you by cleaning your windshields for free."

He gave a classic British response: "Jolly good!" The businessman then went back inside and told the others. Heads were shaking, people were waving, and then some further discussion followed. From the smiles on the customers' faces, this group knew they had succeeded in redefining what it meant to be a Christian. In the eyes of those donut shop customers, Christians were those who debate and ask for donations.

Serving is a catalyst for the kingdom of God to go forward into the world. Our credibility grows as we walk in servanthood, and the greater our authority, the more the world will listen to our message. We have known more of promotion than we have of true authority. Recent Church history tells us that very gifted people don't always wield great power and influence.

Jesus was empowered precisely because He came as a servant. Philippians 2:9-11 tells us the end result: "Therefore God also has highly exalted him and given him the name which is above every name, that at the name of Jesus every knee should bow, of those in heaven, and of those on earth, and of those under the earth, and that every tongue should confess that Jesus Christ is Lord, to the glory of God the Father." As the ultimate servant, Jesus received ultimate authority from the Father. Because He had authority in the lives of those He served, Jesus was able to call people to repentance.

Mother Teresa was one of the most influential people on the earth because she served perhaps more than anyone. Tony Campolo describes Mother Teresa's appearance at a Harvard University chapel service. She didn't pull any punches. At one point she said, "I understand there are lots of you students in this school who are doing things that displease God. You are harming yourselves and offending God. Some of you are drinking alcohol and taking drugs. Others of you are engaged in sexual sin of many sorts. I have a message for you from God: Repent, turn away from what you are doing."

The result of Mother Teresa's exhortation was amazing. The entire auditorium full of people rose to their feet and applauded thunderously for several minutes. They gave this simple woman a standing ovation for calling them to repentance! Her credibility as a servant gave her authority as a speaker.

Servanthood leads to authority and success in the business world as well. According to an article in the *New York Times*, Japanese donut makers have discovered the power of serving through their own experience.

It can be argued that anyone who opens a Mister Donut franchise in Japan really wants to. On the first day of management training, the future entrepreneurs are sent by bus to a Kyoto residential district, where they go from house to house, knocking on doors and politely asking permission to scrub the family toilet. . . . The spirit of thanksgiving is not dead in the Mister Donut operation today—and it also pinpoints the difference between Japan's Mister Donut and its American counterpart. Each year on January 27, the day it was decided to introduce Mister Donut in Japan, every shop manager, sales person, and baker in the Japanese operation is dispatched to clean a public washroom in the spirit of "self-reflection and gratitude," as a company leaflet describes it.[3]

When people express a desire to love as Jesus does, I usually ask them if they are willing to serve others in practical ways, even if they know that person will never come to know Christ. When they're willing to serve without regard for the response, then I know they're beginning to move in the love of God.

4. DOING THE MESSAGE PRECEDES TELLING THE MESSAGE

As I mentioned earlier in the book, our church offered free gift wrapping as an outreach at area malls during many Christmas seasons. During our first year, we wrapped gifts for the two weeks before Christmas and managed to serve and talk to about ten thousand people. Claire, a recently divorced woman, was one of them. Impressed that we wouldn't take any money for our services, she took a card with our fellowship's name, location and service times listed. She thanked us and left.

Shortly after that day at the mall, Claire visited our church. After the service, she told me that she had thoroughly enjoyed herself, then left and didn't return for nearly 18 months. Then suddenly, Claire came back. Since then, she has been making friends and attending our meetings on a regular basis. Once, we asked her to describe to everyone how she had come to our fellowship. Claire stood in front of the congregation and spoke in a soft, quiet voice.

I first learned about this church a couple of years ago when I had my Christmas gifts wrapped at the mall. Because of things that had gone on in my past, I was fearful of Christians and churches in general. If you had attempted to tell me anything about Jesus then, I would have run away as quickly as possible in the opposite direction. Instead, you wrapped my presents for me, you asked how my shopping was going, and you let me see that you cared about me. You did all that without asking for money or anything else. When I saw that, I realized that I didn't need to be afraid anymore.

By serving this woman and putting the ball "back into her court," we opened a door for the Lord to begin working in her heart. That work, Claire says, went on quietly for over a year—until she was "ripe" for harvesting. This divorced mother of two now has a personal relationship with Jesus and is growing from regular fellowship with other believers.

> *"If you had attempted to tell me anything about Jesus then, I would have run away as quickly as possible in the opposite direction. Instead, you wrapped my presents for me, you asked how my shopping was going, and you let me see that you cared about me."*

For too long we have been insensitive to people's readiness to embrace Christ. We have tended to treat everyone as though they are equally open to the idea of becoming a Christian. Yet that's not true. Had we run roughshod over Claire at the wrapping booth, she would have chalked up the experience as another negative encounter with overly excited Christians. Cornering her with information about how she could get right with God would have been what she was expecting, with a head-to-head attempt to overcome all of her reasons for resisting Christ.

At one time, I thought the person with the best argument was declared the winner. After talking to lots of non-Christians over the years, I have come to see that most arguments about the gospel don't go very far in bringing people to Christ. When Christians come across as argumentative, we are often perceived as being unloving and harsh. Those few unbelievers who like to argue are typically going to believe what they want to believe—no matter how persuasive an evangelist happens to be.

I believe that the process of coming to Jesus Christ is more like the concept of falling in love with the person you'll eventually marry. In fact, this metaphor of the Church as the bride and Jesus as the bridegroom runs throughout the New Testament. To this day I have not known anyone who met someone, fell utterly in love, and then married that person all in the space of 15 minutes.

Such a notion of marriage sounds silly to us, but that picture is not too different from what we have assumed in much of our evangelistic efforts.

Each Christian holds what I call an "evangelism equation," a particular view regarding how a person comes to know Jesus personally. This equation greatly influences how we seek to lead people to Christ. As a traditional "soul winner," my evangelism equation went like this:

Telling the message + call to response
= traditional evangelism

This equation typifies most tracts and gospel messages in our day. Our emphasis has clearly been upon telling the gospel to unbelievers. Evangelicals especially have believed that if we can tell the gospel more clearly, then we will be more effective. A brief examination of any number of popular books on evangelism would reflect this strong emphasis on the message aspect of evangelism. I believe we have gotten the story partly right, but by and large have oversimplified the process of leading others to Christ.

The greatest shortfall of this approach is that it cuts out one of our strongest weapons as Christians: the kindness of God. It is one thing to tell the gospel and quite another to communicate, in a meaningful way, the love of God. Telling does not necessarily bring understanding. And telling is not welcomed until hearts are hungry.

Some time ago, I drove by a large evangelical church displaying this sign out front: *God loves you and wants to know you. There, now you can't say later on that you didn't hear it.* This statement is perhaps a little more rugged than what most of us are used to, but we have all been guilty of sending the gospel to others rather than bringing it as Jesus did, from individual to individual and from heart to heart.

Evangelism messages often apply pressure by quoting from 2 Corinthians 6:2: "Now is the day of salvation." Now is the day of salvation *if* that happens to agree with God's timetable for that particular person. What is the Spirit of the Lord doing in the hearts of those we encounter? As Jesus said, "No one can come to me unless the Father who sent me draws him" (John 6:44, *RSV*). Applying human pressure to someone is likely to do more harm than good. I no longer expect that each person I encounter will necessarily agree with the gospel, repent and ask Jesus into his or her heart on the spot. I do, however, expect that something significant is taking place in people's hearts, whether they accept Christ at that moment or not.

Our aim was to make evangelism a part of everything we do. We saw people come into a relationship with Christ in many of our groups and at all of our Sunday meetings—whether we did an altar call or not. People were coming to Christ in the parking lot, in the restrooms, in the hallways and usually at the most unpredictable times. We found that where a spirit of evangelism was welcomed, people came to Christ whether or not evangelism programs were going on.

At our Sunday morning meetings, we sought to touch people with God's love in a variety of ways, beginning the moment they drove into our parking lot. To do this, we had parking lot greeters wear huge sponge hands like those you might see at a football game. These wavers welcomed people as they arrived. To date, we know of two people who have come to know Christ because of this simple act of welcome. One woman kept driving by on Sunday mornings, wondering what kind of church would have wavers stationed in the parking lot. Curiosity got the better of her and she finally stopped in. After several visits, she accepted Jesus into her heart.

From the beginning, our aspiration was to launch a style of evangelism that would become part of our everyday lives. Servant evangelism accomplished just that. Extending God's love to others in practical ways was the key in allowing us to reach people who lived in our community. We discovered over and over that as we came with a heart to serve people—instead of a heart to tell, preach or talk down to them—they were very receptive.

With each act of service that we did around the city of Cincinnati, someone's life was touched—someone who usually went on to tell others about what was done for them in the name of the Lord. In short, when we touched the lives of people where they *really lived*—by lessening their pain and by making their day a little more livable—those people who had been served went on to become walking advertisements for the kingdom of God and for the local church.

I read about a beer company that sponsored a contest to promote summer sales. Certain cans were specially rigged so that opening them triggered a recorded message: "You won!" When we serve others with hearts of love, a little voice is spoken by the Holy Spirit to those we serve: "You are loved! God is real! Come to Me!" Much more than simply being served or receiving something for free, unbelievers experience the presence of God. By receiving the act of love we offer, they unknowingly are inviting the presence of God into their lives. Their hearts are being invaded.

More people than ever are hungry for God. But if we come to unbelievers with a message of "Get right with God or get left," we are forcing them in or out.

More people than ever are hungry for God. But if we come to unbelievers with a message of "Get right with God or get left," we are forcing them in or out. While they may need to come into the Kingdom, it may take some time for them to make the transition. Too often, we try to make people decide for or against the Lord far too early in the process. What we immediately chalk up as a "rejection" of the gospel often should be scored as "incomplete."

Certainly, there is a time and place for a verbal presentation of the gospel. As Paul says, "How shall they hear without a preacher?" (Rom. 10:14). Nevertheless, I believe we have reversed the natural order of evangelism. We need to love with our actions first, and then offer words of love to explain precisely what God's life is all about. Of course we must bring the message of the good news, but confining that message to words alone is a huge mistake. St. Francis said it best: "Wherever you go, preach the gospel, and if necessary, use words."

5. Focus on Planting, Not Harvesting

A woman named Michelle Brandes was led to the Lord by Christian musician Keith Green and went on to serve as his secretary for several years. Considering Michelle's background, this was a strange turn of events for her life. Raised in a Reformed Jewish home in the San Fernando Valley area of Los Angeles, she would have qualified as a "God-fearer," although she had no personal relationship with Jesus.

Keith and his wife, Melody, befriended Michelle until finally one day she invited Jesus Christ into her heart. That would make a great ending to this story, except that nothing apparently happened when Michelle uttered that prayer. Over a period of more than two years, Keith led Michelle in a prayer of repentance an amazing six times!

Some might ask, "Why pray the same prayer so many times when only once is necessary to get through to God?" Keith shared the same basic explanation of the gospel each time, and Michelle prayed the same heartfelt and sincere prayer, but for some reason it didn't "take" until they prayed on the seventh occasion.

Most of the Christians I know would have taken Michelle back to the Scriptures and encouraged her to just believe the truth of God's Word. To quote a famous tract, she should get the train of "fact-faith-feeling" aligned properly. Keith was either smart enough or instinctive enough to keep asking Michelle to pray one more time until somehow she and the Lord got aligned. When in doubt, he kept on planting seeds of faith and love. Most importantly, Keith realized that God is the one doing the real work of evangelism. As we faithfully conduct ourselves as seed planters and waterers, God will complete the work of harvesting.

From a parallel reading of Acts and 1 Corinthians, I believe Paul had his own Howard Beale experience in Athens. Although he was one of the best-educated men of his generation, Paul's trust in his intellect came to a screeching halt one day. According to the account in Acts 17, this famous apostle reasoned with the rich and famous and well-bred intellectual set of Athens.

Paul's track record was impressive. When this man spoke, things usually happened. Yet Luke describes the less than enthusiastic response to Paul's preaching on this particular day: "Paul departed . . . however, some men joined him and believed" (Acts 17:33-34). A few is better than none, but Paul was not used to such a meager response. As he left Athens for Corinth, this great preacher was shaken to the core by his experience. Later he wrote, "I was with you in weakness, in fear, and in much trembling" (1 Cor. 2:3).

After this experience, Paul's entire view of evangelism changed. We all have ideas of what we think will work, but we don't find out what really works until we step out to do it. Paul no longer put his trust in finely crafted words. He said, "My speech and my preaching were not with persuasive words of human wisdom, but in demonstration of the Spirit and of power" (1 Cor. 2:4). Never again would Paul minister with words of persuasion apart from utter dependence on the power of the Holy Spirit for his success in ministry.

Paul now clearly perceived an important truth: Only the Holy Spirit can bring a person to faith. He goes on to make it clear that evangelism is a process: "I have planted, Apollos watered, but God gave the increase. So then neither he who plants is anything, nor he who waters, but God who gives the increase" (1 Cor. 3:6-7). Human beings can play an important role in bringing the good news to others, but it is God alone who is the real evangelist.

When we talk about evangelism, we aren't generally talking about the planting-watering-harvesting cycle that Paul describes. We usually mean the results—the harvest alone. In fact, we have become so completely preoccupied with this last phase of the evangelism process that it has tainted our approach to bringing people to Christ. Sometimes I hear comments like, "How many prayed the prayer?" "How many were baptized?" "How many responded?" "How many did you close the deal with?"

When I would pray with someone to accept Christ, I used to say that "I led the person to the Lord." I no longer use that phrase, because it is inaccurate. We need to understand that we are incapable of leading anyone to Christ whom the Holy Spirit is not already drawing.

Evangelism is a process that begins with planting along the lines of what Paul did. He and others like him would come into towns "not building on other men's work" and speak the basics of the life and gospel of Jesus Christ. Some would listen, some wouldn't. The process continued with the ministry of people like Apollos who watered and nurtured the already-planted seed. At some point God Himself would eventually reap a harvest as someone came to faith in Jesus Christ.

This concept flies in the face of our cultural value for an immediate conclusion. Americans don't tend to value process. At best, we tolerate any delay of gratification. We like closure. We are into results. Our houses are full of products that give testimony to our demand for immediacy and convenience: microwave ovens, remote controls to cable TV with umpteen channels, instant glue that forms a permanent bond in less than a minute.

My last experience in purchasing a car wasn't too different from our typical American approach to evangelism. The salesman turned up the hype and twisted my arm with "for tonight, and tonight only, you can buy this car at this price. But as soon as you walk out the door, that offer is over. And please, if you don't buy tonight, don't tell my boss how ridiculously low I'm going on this vehicle. I could lose my job for giving you such an amazing deal."

I told him that I wasn't interested in buying anything without first thinking it over, looking at our budget, and talking at length with my wife. She wouldn't be happy if I bought a car without consulting her, regardless of the "amazing deal" he was offering me. The salesman was desperate to close the deal while I was still in an information-gathering phase.

No sales manager gets excited when one of his struggling salespeople reports, "Well, I didn't make any actual sales this month, but I talked to a lot of people who are considering buying from us in the future." The typical response would be, "Who cares about *considering* buying from us. I want some closed deals and I want them now!"

I fear our cultural values of instant response and the bottom line have produced a distinctly American form of evangelism.

I fear our cultural values of instant response and the bottom line have produced a distinctly American form of evangelism. When was the last time you heard someone get excited about planting seeds of God's love? Our evangelistic efforts are too often met with the question, "So, how many people prayed to accept Christ?" If the number is low, we automatically feel disappointed and mutter, "Oh well, I tried."

That attitude is far from the one Paul took. Though he saw some people immediately accept Christ, the general response to Paul's message in Athens was lackluster. If he evaluated the fruit of his ministry on the response of that particular day, he probably would have given up early on. Fortunately Paul was able to see evangelism as a process—one that God Himself is overseeing in each case. Paul also recognized his own vital and distinct role, even if he didn't get to see each planted seed come to fullness of faith.

C. S. Lewis, in his autobiography, *Surprised by Joy*, tells of struggling for months with the gospel. Somehow he couldn't get past the "unreasonableness" of the message. Lewis's story seems to me not too different from that of another famous British intellect, Bertrand Russell. Both of these men asked the same questions and came up with the same unsatisfactory answers early in life. Both describe a tremendous struggle with the gospel, of how they got into the issues of the gospel, dissected them point by point, but still could not come to belief. Although they asked many of the same questions, their conclusions were very different. Russell wrote of his struggle and conclusion that God is not real in his book *Why I Am Not a Christian*.

Lewis's story took a significant turn one day, almost to his surprise. The arena for battle shifted from his head to his heart. As he tells it, he was on the back of his brother's motorcycle on his way to the zoo. He says, "All that I know is that when I got on that motorcycle I did not believe in Jesus and that by the time we arrived at the zoo I was a believer."[4] When we rightly understand evangelism, we recognize that it is both a miracle and a mystery how any of us come to know Christ.

I personally saw a man whose heart was opened to the good news of Jesus Christ after it had been softened by the kindness of God. This happened when I was in Las Vegas doing an evangelism seminar. Typically when I speak at a conference for a couple of evenings, I also organize several outreaches into the community. After hearing about evangelism, we always need to go one step further and actually do it!

On this particular Saturday, we put together a free Coke giveaway and washed windshields at several locations around town. At Sunday services on the following day, a young guy in his mid-twenties walked into the meeting carefully carrying an empty Coke can. He had a somewhat glazed look on his face. One of the regulars went over to meet him and offered to throw away the can for him.

"Oh no, I'm not going to throw away this can. I'm saving this can. You see, *this* is the can of Coke that the Christians gave me yesterday in order to *show me God's love.*"

I don't know that man's full story, but it is clear that the simple act of giving away a cold drink at a stoplight in a conversation that only lasted 10 seconds had made a significant impact on him. I believe that this man came much closer to having a relationship with Christ as a result of the kindness showed him. I don't know whether he accepted Christ that Sunday, but I do believe that he is well on his way toward knowing Christ in a personal and dynamic way. Even though I am the writer of this book, I am not the author of this man's story. Only God knows how his story is going to end.

When we rightly understand evangelism, we recognize that it is both a miracle and a mystery how any of us come to know Christ.

Several years ago I would have been disappointed that I was not able to "close the deal" with this man, that he had slipped away. I would have felt somewhat guilty that I didn't get him to pray the sinner's prayer right there at the meeting. I don't feel that pressure anymore because I know God Himself is overseeing this process, not me. It was obvious this man has a heart inclined toward God. As long as he is asking the right questions, it's probably just a matter of time until he makes a commitment to Christ.

Am I disappointed when people don't respond? Hardly ever, because I know from lots of experiences that each person I meet is being worked on by the drawing power of the Holy Spirit. My joyful task is simply to bump them forward a notch or two through practical acts of love and service.

MORE KINDNESS

Above all else, desire to care about others. We live in a time when life is lived at far, far too fast a rate for any of us to keep up and still remain human. We have become rabbits in a life designed by God for turtles.

Let's return to being turtles as God created us.

So many of the promises Jesus offered us are possible only as we leave the rabbit life behind and begin to live as the turtles He created us to be. He speaks of His sheep being able to hear His voice and to know His name. Sorry for the shameless mixing of animal metaphors, but rabbits on the run don't hear much besides "Run for your life! The dogs are after us!"

To slow down and be sheep (or turtles!), we start with the simple desire to care. We ask God in our heart of hearts, "I want to care. Reshape my heart so that I can care." The desire to live out of a deep place of care is the only way we can live the lives Jesus calls us to. If we do not live out of care, we will not come close to being fulfilled. To offer joyful, selfless care is a desire God has planted deep in each of our hearts—we are called to live on behalf of others. We have a deep desire to serve them with all of our hearts, and we cannot know fulfillment until we walk in that lifestyle.

Notes
1. St. John of the Cross, *Dark Night of the Soul* (New York: Image, Doubleday, 1959).
2. Gayle D. Erwin, *The Jesus Style* (Waco, TX: Word, 1983), p. 146.
3. Abridged from T. Trucco, "Serving Mr. Donut and the Community," *The New York Times*, December 26, 1982.
4. C. S. Lewis, *Surprised by Joy* (New York: Inspirational, 1987), p. 130.

CHAPTER 6

Ready, *Fire*, Aim!

*A knowledge of the path cannot be substituted for putting
one foot in front of the other.*
M. C. RICHARDS

Give light, and the darkness will disappear of itself.
ERASMUS

When I first arrived in Cincinnati, I started getting together
with several other men every Saturday for breakfast. Eventually
our group added a Bible study. Our coziness was disrupted one
week when the designated leader chose the topic of God's love
for the poor as portrayed by the Minor Prophets. These inspired
authors connect the coming of God's presence with His people
stepping out to meet the needs of those who are hurting.

We desperately wanted to see God's presence in our midst,
so we decided to make a leap of faith. Taking our Bible study
one step further into a "Bible do," we began to put into practice
God's written love for people by reaching out to those in need.
Our men's group would typically eat breakfast, do a brief Bible
study and then go out to do ministry. That began a tradition in
our church of using Saturday mornings as a time for giving of
ourselves to serve others in a practical way.

Our commitment to "Bible dos" forced us to move from
theory to practice in our Christian lives. We will never be truly

ready. We will forever be growing in our knowledge of how to evangelize more effectively, but we mustn't stipulate that our training process be complete before we begin to obey the Lord. If we wait until we have full understanding, we will never get out of the starting block.

Our commitment to "Bible dos"
forced us to move from theory to
practice in our Christian lives.

Our motto for several years was "Ready, *Fire*, Aim!" I have heard critics say, "That sounds reckless." Perhaps. Nevertheless, I vote to just get started—whether we feel ready or not. In my many years as a pastor, I have seen too many Christians remain in the preparation mode without ever putting into action what they've been preparing to do. I heard Billy Graham once say at a crusade, "God has a difficult time guiding a rocket before it is launched. Get off the launching pad and guidance will come to you." Let's take a closer look in this chapter at the practicalities of launching out into servant evangelism.

PLAN, BUT PLAN AS YOU GO

I'm amazed at the number of people who come up to me at conferences and ask, "But how do you actually just start doing this?"

I usually respond by asking another question: "What's so difficult about cleaning a windshield? I can show you my technique, then you need to get out there and do it." The basic idea behind these servant evangelism projects is very simple. It's not that difficult to begin loving people in practical ways. We need to avoid the human tendency to make things overly complicated.

We often use planning as an excuse for not doing. Many times we're just waiting for someone to invite us into the game or waiting for someone in authority to give us permission to serve others in Jesus' name. It seems to me that permission has already been granted numerous times by Jesus and by those inspired by the Holy Spirit to write His words in Scripture.

I'm not against planning in the least. The Bible specifically tells us that "we should make plans . . . counting on God to direct us" (Prov. 16:9). We also read, "A prudent man foresees the difficulties ahead and prepares for them" (Prov. 22:3). But we often take such caution too far in order to avoid taking risks. In many respects the church seems to prefer being expert *planners* rather than expert *doers*. That's why I say, "Plan as you go." Plan to the extent necessary, but don't go overboard.

While planning at its worst can be a crutch for not doing, a lack of planning will result in frustration and inefficiency for all concerned. Clearly we need to balance planning with the execution of those plans. The leadership in our church planned out events for a quarter of the year at a time. Our plans kept us on track and honest, but the key was always sticking to those plans as much as possible.

START SIMPLE

Begin by working on projects that are inexpensive and don't require a lot of preparation time. Appendix 1 lists about 70 projects that we have used with some degree of success. With your own resources in mind, look for the ones that would be the easiest to accomplish without much preparation.

One week, a local food chain donated 1,000 cartons of eggs to our church. We had never given away eggs but figured that most people eat them, so we planned to give them away door to door as a service project. Several small groups went into the community and gave one or two dozen eggs to each household. Two people said, "Funny you should stop by with eggs! I was just on my way out the door to buy eggs."

It doesn't take a lot of organization to pull off a successful project. Something as simple as eggs and eager people willing to knock on a few doors can make a huge impact on your community. Start with very simple projects with few moving parts. Later, after you have some successes under your belt, you can tackle the more complicated ones.

Something is always better than nothing, but ideally when you launch out into servant evangelism, do several projects in quick succession to get your feet wet. If I had six people going out, I would choose two different projects right off that didn't require a lot of people power.

As you continue to gain experience, lots of different kinds of projects need to be available. Outreach is sort of like fishing. Fish bite in every kind of weather depending on the bait you use and the kind of fish you want to catch. Some sort of "catch" needs to be happening when you go out to do ministry. On a given day, split up into three groups with an attitude of "We'll catch something if we try several approaches." If washing windshields doesn't work for some reason, maybe feeding parking meters will go over. If neither of those works, try cleaning toilets.

IDENTIFY THE PAINS OF YOUR CITY

God knows the hearts and needs of your community. Ask Him to reveal those specific needs to you as you step out to serve. He promises to reveal Himself to us if we seek Him: "Call to me, and I will answer you, and show you great and mighty things, which you do not know" (Jer. 33:3).

A huge key to success in reaching out to your city is having a grasp on local pressure points. What proves to be an effective outreach project in Seattle may not work so well in Omaha. Fortunately, God cherishes the people of both places and is perfectly capable of showing us how we can creatively enter their lives. The very best and most creative outreach projects for your community are ones that you will probably discover as you do service projects.

We live in a needy world. Their need is our open door for touching their hearts. The question is simply, "Given our present resources and boundaries, what could we do to touch these people with God's kingdom in a practical way?" God has more creative ideas than we could exhaust in a million lifetimes of ministry. Tap into His mind and take notes.

One way to receive God's guidance involves simply looking around you. Each person struggles with the pain of life. Ultimately all human pain stems from our alienation from God, but some types are unique to specific communities. In what specific ways do those who live in your city need help, healing and wholeness? As we discover those particular needs and begin to meet them, we quickly gain credibility and a receptive audience.

For a number of years, mail carriers from the north side of Cincinnati used our church parking lot as a spot for coffee breaks. One day, another pastor and I went out washing windshields and decided to wash the windows of the mail truck parked at the edge of our lot. The carrier instantly opened up with us by asking if we would pray for his mother who had terminal brain cancer. We were able to interact at a deeper level in that five-minute conversation than we would have over years of passing him and saying, "Hi . . . bye."

When I first came to Christ, I was much more sensitive to the pain of life around me because I too was hurting. After years of soaking up God's abundant love and healing, I began to not notice others' pain so much. I became a lot like the priest and Levite who passed by the man in the ditch. I could see with my eyes but yet walk right past and not take to heart the trauma of those in need. As we seek to reach out to our communities, it's time we noticed that pain once again.

Some of my best ideas for outreach projects have come to me as I strolled through the local mall with a cup of coffee in my hand and simply watched those who passed by.

How do you identify the pain of the people in your city? If you have no idea where to begin, simply spend a couple of hours walking around a local mall. Look into the eyes of those who pass by. Ask yourself and God, "How do they hurt? What could I realistically do to relieve some of the difficulties they're experiencing?" I believe you will receive new insights.

Some of my best ideas for outreach projects have come to me as I strolled through the local mall with a cup of coffee in my hand and simply watched those who passed by. They all have a bundle of needs. A popular cartoon captures the current predicament of most people. One woman tells a coworker, "Most of the people I know are on the verge of hysteria 24 hours a day, and they're the lucky ones. Everyone else *is* hysterical all the time."

Consider actually asking people at the mall their opinion. You could introduce yourself and say, "I'm a Christian. I want to do something practical for the people of this community. What do you think I could do?" I have also posed this same question in another way: "If Jesus Christ were here today and offered to help you, what would you ask of Him?" You will have some enlightening conversations on your hands!

WHEN STARTING OUT, PAY YOUR OWN WAY AS MUCH AS POSSIBLE

I'm often asked, "How do you pay for these outreach projects?" From the beginning, our local fellowship assigned 15 percent of its total income to evangelism and ministry to the poor. For an established church that hasn't had an outreach fund, this idea may seem impractical. Yet if the church holds evangelism as a value, eventually we must assign money to express that value. I challenge pastors to become financially committed to reaching out to those outside the church, but I realize that it takes time to go from zero percent of a budget to a significant allowance.

If you have no funds for getting started, consider pooling a bit of your own money. If you're in a small group, put your money together and invest in some supplies. With just $10 you can buy a couple of good squeegees, some Windex, and you're on your way! Perhaps it would be appropriate to put on a fundraiser to gather funds for purchasing equipment. Maybe the local missions fund could be tapped into. After all, this certainly qualifies as local missions!

Most of the projects we did in servant evangelism are actually very affordable. Sometimes for literally just a few dollars, many people can be touched in a practical way. For example, one project we liked to do was to go door to door with 60-watt light bulbs and offer to replace any burned-out ones. When purchased in bulk, light bulbs cost very little yet provide an entry point into the lives of each family.

REPORT TO YOUR PASTORS, BUT DON'T PUT EXPECTATIONS UPON THEM

I encourage you to take the slow route in getting your pastor involved in servant evangelism. Most pastors I know are already overextended. The best way to get their positive attention is to do a couple of projects on your own and then report back to them with your results. Pastors are always looking for a workable approach that can get the average person involved in evangelism. Although no long-term outreach program will be established without some sort of pastoral leadership, your personal enthusiasm for these projects needs to be shared with patience, wisdom and tact.

After pastoring for several decades now, I know that the spontaneous direction of my responsibilities revolves around reacting to internal problems. Evangelism falls under the category of *"pro*action" rather than "*re*action." At least in a small and perhaps symbolic way, I believe that pastors need to get out into the community on a regular basis. If we don't schedule these ventures into our busy lives, we will simply cave in to the pressures of day-to-day church life and perpetuate an unhealthy pattern of inwardness.

Pastors obviously have a deep love for non-Christians, but the ministry of pastoring can easily separate and isolate them.

My own informal surveys indicate that less than 5 percent of pastors consistently spend time around the nonchurched. Servant evangelism provides necessary reality therapy because it gets them out into the real world. Besides, ultimately Christians will do only what their pastors do. I required all of the staff members of our church to participate in some sort of evangelism outing at least once per month. I also required all pastors on our staff to go out every other week. We were all very busy and could easily justify not doing so, but then we could easily get stuck in a little circle chasing our own tails.

A pastor in downtown Denver told me about his experience of putting on a Matthew's Party for the needy. Church members fed people, played games, led square dancing, and had a wonderful time. This pastor had even arranged for several of the players from the Denver Nuggets basketball team to take part. After the party had ended, they tallied up well over a thousand people who had attended.

This pastor broke down weeping while describing his experience, "I talked to more unchurched people today than I have in the past several years combined." Pastors obviously have a deep love for non-Christians, but the *ministry* of pastoring can easily separate and isolate them. We must resist the trend of giving aid to fellow believers and yet never spending time with people outside of our local fellowships.

ADDING WORDS TO YOUR DEEDS

What we say to explain our actions in servant evangelism is obviously of great importance. Since we put most of the stress on the deed being done, the few words we share ought to be carefully considered. This is the basic phrase we use to explain ourselves: "We're doing a free community service project to show God's love in a practical way."

As I have already mentioned, the simple word "free" holds great power. Unfortunately, most of the time it is used with some sort of catch. When the church youth group offers a "free" car wash, they really mean, "Donations are gladly accepted!" Door-to-door projects often elicit a jaded look from those who answer. "Yeah, right, I'm sure it's free . . . so what do you want from me?" When we reassure them that there's no catch—that we are serving just for the joy of serving and showing God's love—people are often blown away! "You mean to tell me this is really free?"

When we use the important phrase "community service project," we are putting ourselves in the same league as the Kiwanis, Lions Club and Boy Scouts. I don't consider this to be any sort of subterfuge. We are truly serving the community as we reach out in servant evangelism.

"Showing God's love in a practical way" is the evangelistic clause in our explanation. We have found this pregnant phrase especially effective in getting our foot in the door of the lives and hearts of those we serve. I have also found it fairly easy to go from those few words to a more in-depth conversation regarding Christ.

I encourage you to use this phrase exactly as I have shared it, at least when starting out in servant evangelism. Of course, you may find more effective ways of communicating this same message as you go along. Regardless of the phrase you use, it's important that you say a lot with just a few words. Remember, our goal is to encounter a lot of ships passing in the night while leaving them with something to think about afterward.

COMMIT YOURSELF TO A MINIMUM OF SIX MONTHS OF DOING PROJECTS

It takes time to see the results of servant evangelism. I recommend that you not seriously evaluate your results until you have been doing such projects for six months. The common tendency is to begin reaching out and then to immediately evaluate the daylights out of the little bit of practice we've gotten.

On the other hand, I do recommend that you keep track of the numbers of people you serve from week to week. This record will be a helpful motivator when it seems as though you're not making any headway. We can rejoice periodically with the thought, *With this many being served, surely some significant seeds are being planted in hearts through us.* We don't want to get stuck in a numbers game of notching our Bibles for each person we evangelize, but we do have to maintain our motivation and enthusiasm.

I encourage you to make it your goal to create an "atmosphere of evangelism" more than to run a program. Building such an atmosphere will take time. Good things will be sown from your first outing, but it will take time to begin to see the fruit of your labor. Typically it takes six months for a local church to catch on to this new approach to evangelism.

COULD I ASK YOU A QUESTION?

People who are initially exploring this idea of servant evangelism usually have a lot of questions. The following are a sampling of the ones I commonly hear. Hopefully they will address some of your concerns.

What's So Different About Servant Evangelism?
In a nutshell, the uniqueness of this approach to sharing the good news can be described in this way:

1. It's quick.
2. It's high volume.
3. It's done in groups.
4. It's culture-current.
5. It gives the Holy Spirit an open door to convict those we are leading to Christ.
6. It allows shy people to launch into effective evangelism.
7. It's an approach that Christian families can do together.
8. It's easily picked up by new Christians.
9. It's simple.
10. It's friendly, non-pushy and nonaggressive.
11. It appeals to every segment of our cities by providing many specific projects from which to choose.

12. It's emotionally safe for those who have been trauma-
    tized by negative experiences with evangelism.
13. It's giving-centered rather than asking-centered.
14. It provides a safe place for ambitious people to expend
    their energy.
15. It provides an open door for the miraculous—if God so
    moves.
16. It's big fun!

How Does Servant Evangelism Fit In with Other Approaches?
God is ultimately overseeing the process of evangelism in each
person's life. We are the seed flingers; He is the Master Gar-
dener. God uses numerous connections to bring new children
into His family. I am continually amazed at the diverse stories
of conversion I hear from new believers.

Every person is at a unique place in his or her gradual awak-
ening to the love of Christ. Servant evangelism draws everyone
it touches closer to accepting Christ regardless of his or her own
personal situation. In some cases we will be making initial contact with people who have never interacted with a Christian. At
other times we will be watering the seeds already sown by others.

*By itself, servant evangelism is incomplete as
an approach to sharing the gospel. Traditional
approaches alone are also incomplete.*

By itself, servant evangelism is incomplete as an approach
to sharing the gospel. Traditional approaches alone are also
incomplete. By focusing on the earlier phases of planting and
watering, deeds of kindness tenderize hearts so that they can
later receive the message of God's love. I don't believe servant

evangelism will work unless we also use more traditional approaches to actually harvest those accepting Christ. As we serve people, God will provide opportunities to explain the gospel message and eventually pray a sinner's prayer with someone. Many useful aids have been developed for this purpose, including *Evangelism Explosion*, the *Four Spiritual Laws*, and *Steps to Peace with God*.

How Do People Respond When Served?

Our service projects usually drew some sort of response, often in the form of inquiries about our church. One of the most often-asked questions was, "How long do your services last?" Others who were looking for a Bible-based fellowship asked, "Does your church believe in the Bible?"

Other responses varied. People in a good mood tended to react with surprise and gratefulness. Big-city people—who were often more skeptical—wondered what we were up to and what we wanted from them. They also tended to be in a hurry most of the time, so we had to gear our projects to their pace. We touched just a small percentage of people while they were in an open frame of mind. These individuals sometimes would talk at length with us. When we had a chance to openly chat with folks, it seemed that about 5 percent were open to coming to Christ right there on the spot!

What Are the Most Typical Questions People Ask?

Some of the most common questions we heard people ask were the following:

"Who are you people anyway?"
"What are you selling?"
"What's the name of your church?"
"What time do you meet?"

"How long do your services last?"

"Can I make a donation?"

"What do you believe?"

"Are you the kind of Christians that believe in prayer?"

I find it interesting that we heard very few theological questions. Hardly ever did someone ask exactly what we believed.

Will People Be Frightened or Offended?

Responses vary greatly, but in our experience people rarely became overtly upset with us. A friend of mine in New York City has been reaching out with servant evangelism projects for a few years now. He has washed literally thousands of windshields in arguably the world's least friendly city. To date, he has received only one negative response, surprisingly from two women with a big Bible on the dashboard! They shooed him away before he could get a word in edgewise.

Use the word "free" with a big smile and almost all of the negative responses will be eliminated.

When people are frightened, it is usually because they don't know how to respond to such an unusual offer. I have found the best way to put someone at ease is simply to put on the biggest smile you can muster. Smiles are incredibly disarming. One time, I was going from car to car washing windshields in a mall parking lot. I was about half finished with one car when I saw three big college-aged guys running toward me. Their look of suspicion turned to laughter when I turned around smiling. They said they thought I might have been breaking into their car, but then they thanked me enthusiastically and went their way.

Simply making good eye contact is another helpful way to let people know that they have nothing to fear. Looking confident will also convince potential critics that we are okay. When any kind of tension develops, I find it very helpful to mention the word "free" as quickly as possible. Having been conditioned to requests for donations, people automatically expect us to ask for something in return for our service. Use the word "free" with a big smile and almost all of the negative responses will be eliminated. When we went door to door, residents were sometimes fearful to the point of not wanting to open their doors to us. They would often yell, "Who is it?" through the closed door. Usually I yelled back, "I'm Steve. We're giving away great free stuff." That usually overcame their resistance.

What Negative Responses Do You Get?

We usually sought the minimal amount of permission when we did projects. When it seemed appropriate, we even washed windshields or plugged parking meters of unattended cars. On occasion, people would walk up as we were washing their windshield and say, "Hey, stay away from my car!" However, they usually expressed appreciation once they heard our explanation.

Sometimes, people assumed that we were selling something. Especially in busy downtown areas where a lot of panhandlers are operating, many of those who passed by were afraid of making eye contact with a stranger. One of our small groups was comprised of business people who worked in downtown Cincinnati. About once a month, this group would do some sort of outreach to other business people in a center section called Fountain Square. Usually, they gave away gourmet coffee, washed windshields or cleaned toilets for area businesses. The group leader reported that they gained increasing credibility from the typically skeptical business people as they continued serving in these ways.

In any single project, we found some measure of rejection to our offer to serve. Whether we were giving away Cokes or raking leaves or refilling bird feeders, some people gave us a curt no with little explanation. We were not disappointed when this happened, however, because we consistently saw that the power of what we were doing wasn't confined to the particular product or service we offered but simply the idea that we were doing this to show God's love. That offer is so powerful that it really does unsettle people when they consider it.

For months, we cleaned the front windows of an Ohio State liquor store. The manager's first response to our offer to wash his windows for free was, "Sure it's free this time, but how much will it be next time?" We never took money from anyone for any of our projects, and this man was no exception. After five or six months of serving this man, we found ourselves on a first-name basis. He even once confided in us that he had re-turned to the church he grew up in after being gone for several years—all because we had begun to serve him. Our offer was spurned at first, but the invitation had an eventual effect.

We realize before we even set foot outside of the church parking lot that a certain percentage of our seeds of kindness will be rejected.

We typically experienced about a 50 percent rejection rate on our first offer to clean people's toilets. About the worst that happened was that we were denied permission, with the usual reason being that the employee wanted to check with the boss. Sometimes the person was so shocked they didn't know what to say. When we were denied permission, we usually offered to come back some other time to do something practical. Then we made it a point to return to that same home or business a couple of weeks later. Usually, we weren't turned down the second time around.

How Do You Deal with Rejection?

We realized before we even set foot outside of the church parking lot that a certain percentage of our seeds of kindness would be rejected. Some people will say no to just about anything offered them in life. I have met certain people who seem to walk through life with a big NO written across their faces.

Surfers describe a wave that is almost too rough to ride as being "gnarly." I have discovered that a certain percentage of the population goes through life with a consistently gnarly attitude. These folks are mad most of the time. Those who did reject our offer were usually mad before we ever talked to them. If we were to give out $50 bills as a servant evangelism project, they would have probably rejected our offer. These types of people are being worked on by the grace of God, but they probably aren't ripe for harvesting.

One summer on a hot Friday afternoon, we were giving away soft drinks to motorists on their way home from work. One woman was furious at us for approaching her car at all. She yelled, "How dare you offer me a drink! I'm calling the police as soon as I get home because I know for certain this is illegal." Apparently, she was having a rough day. We did nothing to irritate her; she didn't even know who we were, and yet she was mad at us.

We didn't allow this woman's rejection to stop us or even to slow us down. We continued on to the next driver with as big a smile as we could muster. Coincidentally, the next car happened to be a police cruiser. He gladly took a diet drink, thanked us and commented, "This project is a wonderful idea. More churches ought to do this sort of thing."

In short, we didn't take rejection personally. We weren't spending enough time with people or doing anything to elicit rejection. They didn't even know us, so how could they be rejecting *us*? If they did refuse, they were actually rejecting the offer of kindness.

Our job as bringers of God's kingdom is to find the people who are open and invite them into God's family. With those who aren't ready to respond, we should just smile and keep going. The important point to remember is that we can't let a negative response scare us away from the next person—someone who is likely to be more open.

It's impossible to know what's going on inside of those with whom we interact, but I have a theory about those who go ballistic at our offer. I believe that many people in this category are being worked on by the power of the Holy Spirit and that we happen to be one more point along the way before they finally come into a relationship with Jesus Christ. Somehow, our presence as representatives of God irritates them, and they react in anger. Paul the apostle, for example, was at his most violent just before his conversion on the road to Damascus (see Acts 9:1-9).

We need to trust that God will redeem every episode of rejection. Don't forget the inherent power of the offer we are making. We once had a crew cleaning toilets in a local mall. At one store, the employee running the cash register said, "I don't know if you should. It's probably okay, but I'd better ask the boss first. Please come back next Saturday." When the team returned the following week, the employee reported that not only was the owner willing to let our team clean but also that when the boss heard that we had come to clean the toilets, he began to openly weep. This employee admitted, "I've never seen him get emotional at anything. He was really touched by your offer to help us!"

What Activities Don't Work Well?

We had our share of failures. However, we viewed each mistake as an opportunity to grow in our effectiveness as servants. Most of our failures were actually great ideas that just needed a little adjustment or fine-tuning. Here are some of the more creative failures we experienced:

- *Accidentally filling a radiator with windshield washing fluid.* The washer reservoir looks a lot like the radiator reservoir! We paid the $50 to have the woman's radiator flushed.

- *Washing the windshield of an already clean car.* We later paid to have the car washed again.

- *Washing the windshield of a car with a couple of dogs inside.* The dogs were hyperactive and went berserk, doing some damage to the interior. We agreed to pay for damages, but the owner never followed up on our offer.

- *Accidentally setting off car alarms.* Sometimes a sensitive alarm would go off when we lifted a wiper to clean the windshield. Even though this happened dozens of times, we only had one negative encounter with a man who appeared to be in a big hurry and counted us as an inconvenience to his tight schedule. Typically, when people came to check out what happened, they were relieved to see that we were simply there to serve them. We always looked for stickers indicating a car alarm, but not all cars post such a warning. Our rule of thumb was to stay away from vehicles that appeared to be newer or more expensive. We never had the owner of an older car get angry at us for serving him or her!

If we weren't failing on a regular basis, then I assumed that we weren't taking enough risks. A growing list of failure stories indicated to me that we were in a place of balance between prudence and activism.

What Are the Immediate Results of Doing Servant Evangelism?

First, and most importantly, non-Christians will begin to open their hearts to God's love. People are a lot like porcupines: They either turn to us with their soft, vulnerable side or their prickly, skeptical side that says, "I don't want to hear anything about this Jesus you are talking about." A free car wash in New York City prompted one "porcupine" to turn his soft side to us. This man worked for the sanitation department. When he drove into our car wash, he was angry and disgusted because we had caused a traffic slowdown on his route.

The driver of the garbage truck shook his head and muttered, "When I get back to the garage, I just know the other guys aren't gonna believe this happened."

This emotionally charged encounter changed instantly when we offered to wash his entire garbage truck for free. Before he could say no, we were eagerly serving him. This man stood in stunned silence just shaking his head. A couple of the girls standing by explained to him that we just wanted to show him God's love in a practical way. The driver of the garbage truck muttered, "When I get back to the garage I just know the other guys aren't gonna believe this happened." A few minutes later he asked for prayer for a number of issues in his life—right in the middle of the Big Apple's hustle and hurry.

Second, Christians will be built up in their courage to share their faith with unbelievers. I've found that about 50 percent of Christians have shared their faith at some point, but only about 20 percent have actually prayed to lead someone to Christ. Servant evangelism serves as a type of "baby step" toward more risky approaches. As fearful Christians meet unbelievers in a safe, nonconfrontational setting where they experience success, they will gradually grow in their ability to tell others what Jesus has done for them.

What Are the Long-Term Results of Doing Servant Evangelism?
First, the Church will become oriented toward action. The Church is in continual need of redefining. It seems clear that the Church in America is living in an age of great inwardness. One week, I received a monthly catalog from one of the largest Christian book distributors in the country. Out of the 1,000 titles, only 5 concerned evangelism and outreach. About 2 dozen books addressed the challenge of raising teenagers, about 100 dealt with codependency issues, and about 50 discussed the end times.

In light of this inward focus, we need to ask the question, "Why does the Church exist?" We certainly exist to worship God and to grow in wholeness and Christlikeness, but Jesus made it clear that we must also give of ourselves if we hope to keep growing. The Great Commission links God's special presence to the action of the Church going into the world. "Go therefore and make disciples . . . and lo, I am with you always" (Matt. 28:19-20, *RSV*). God is with us in an immediate sense as we carry His life into the world.

Human nature always points the emotional compass inward. To be the Church, we must on occasion grab that compass and point it outward. Jesus promised that "rivers of living water" would flow out of the hearts of all who believe in Him. Try as we may, God will not bless any attempt to make a stagnant and cloistered pond of that river of life. As we bring the

kingdom of God into the community, we will change the world
in which we live.

Second, the church will be redefined to the surrounding community.
The Church in general has taken a lot of blows over the last several years, especially in the wake of scandals involving sex and
money. The world has falsely pictured the entire Church as beg-
gars always on the verge of going out of business. We've also
been pegged as hucksters always looking to get something for
nothing. The third picture the watching world has of the Church
is that of a monastery whose residents have only one message:
"Come in and join us." The world isn't looking to be part of a
failing cause. They want nothing to do with fast-talking, slick
approaches.

As we begin to do humble acts of service in the community,
we will restate our identity. Instead of separatists who are constantly judging the world, we must extend forgiveness, acceptance and love from God. New definitions are slow to catch on,
but hard work will get their attention. We become viable in the
eyes of the world as we get beyond ourselves and serve our way
into their hearts. In an age when the Church has been judged by
the world as being irrelevant and out of touch with people's very
real needs and pains, we prove ourselves worthy of trust.

*Third, the community will be saturated with the presence of these
deeds of kindness.* The word "saturate" may seem like an odd word
to use in reference to evangelism, but it seems to fit when you
consider the long-term effect of this approach. Cincinnati may
have been an exception to the general rule, but it suggests the
level of potential impact. We did servant evangelism projects
consistently for years, expanding our outreach each year. One
year, we directly touched about 100,000 people in greater Cincinnati. Add to that the other congregations in the city who
were doing these outreaches, and the total number touched
was in the neighborhood of 120,000.

The 1993 population of the Cincinnati area was 1.75 million. That means we were approaching the point of touching one-tenth of the city each year. Of course, we encountered many people more than once during a year, but we were still touching a significant part of the city each year. As efforts to serve more and more people continue, 10 or even 20 percent of the city will be touched per year. Over a several year period, huge numbers of the population could be touched.

Aren't Service Projects Really Just to Advertise Your Church?
I can honestly say that ours weren't. Our outreach often led to growth as a side benefit, but we knew that we would lose our integrity if growth were our reason for serving. Such an attitude would also rob the service of its power in people's lives. We weren't giving of ourselves to get anything. Even if we stopped growing altogether, we would continue to serve just as consistently. We must serve for the sake of our own spiritual health. Growth, which seems predictable, must be viewed as serendipity.

We aren't giving of ourselves to get anything.
Even if we stopped growing altogether, we would
continue to serve just as consistently.

As we go about loving with no strings attached, God seems to attach a string of some sort to those actions. He seems to create a tie between the person we serve and Himself. Our prayer in going out into the community was often, "Oh God, let them forget us, but let them never forget You!"

As we served with a good heart, God sent people to us—many of whom we had never served! A spiritual siphon drew people into our church. Even with very little advertising going on, we might have about 5,000 people visit us in a year, 60 percent of whom were unchurched. In summary, you might ask, "You mean that as we serve and *don't* go out of our way to make our church known in the community, that God is going to bring people to us anyway?" That's exactly what we saw in Cincinnati.

MORE KINDNESS

The Words of Life: "Go and do."

Today it is trendy to use words such as "missional," "outward," "outreach." These supposedly describe very old and true ideas that were launched by the God of the Bible from the very beginning of His dealings with man. From the moment Adam and Eve left the Garden, God began to make clear reference to His plan; His heart to gather in those who didn't yet "get it." Christ-followers who follow this track today are sometimes called "emergent."

I have read many if not nearly all of the books that focus on the emergent genre on the market today. I appreciate the books that challenge us as parts of the Church to move outwardly. My encouragement is that we not simply think great thoughts and think of new ways to explain things on PowerPoint, but that we actually do things (such as going outside beyond the four walls of the church) in obedience. Of the books that use the terms "missional," "outward" and "outreach," there is a lot of discussion and challenge to think differently, but little to no stories about what has worked or what is currently working anywhere. Thus, discussion, discussion, discussion.

In the words of the spectacular evangelist of the late 1800s, D.L. Moody, "I like what I'm doing better than what you aren't doing." It's all about what we do . . . or don't do. In Matthew 25,

Jesus said that would help us distinguish the real from the unreal: Those who live the message out and those who simply think curious thoughts. Jesus wasn't one bit cute. He was a profound doer. Let's walk in His footprints all of our days.

There is an amazing amount of fear gripping the Western Church today. That fear is born out of a possibility of failure. The equation goes like this: Risk = Possible Failure = Criticism. Those who follow this equation believe that if we really love the Lord, we won't rock the boat much. We will keep things going forward on an even keel. We won't introduce many—or any—strong ideas.

Note that as you get involved in a lifestyle of kindness and generosity, momentum will most likely begin to follow you as you have never experienced it before. To prepare for this momentum, think through how you will deal with what is inevitably going to come—politics. Certain people will seek to use you to build their own personal kingdom. That kingdom may look similar, but it is not the kingdom of God.

When you joined the Church, perhaps you thought you were getting involved in a politics-free zone. I'm sorry to break the news to you, but you were naive. Many who join in living the kindness focus/generosity invitation tend to be political nincompoops. Guess what? To live that way is perfectly okay! To become political is to compromise the powerful Jesus thing building in your heart. You can't be a constant seed flinger *and* work the system.

But don't be surprised when your refusal to play political games doesn't win you any friends. When Jesus was invited to work the system, He flatly refused—and the insider political system became angrier at His response than anything else Jesus did or said.

Since the writing of *Conspiracy of Kindness*, I have gone through more than one political evisceration. Each one I saw coming from a distance, but I chose to stay committed to the

larger, more valuable issue: how to move the Kingdom forward.
Politics come and go. Current situations rise, fall and are constantly evolving. I urge you to concentrate on the better thing—
that which will endure.

CHAPTER 7

Nuts and Bolts

Charity is the bone shared with the dog when you are
just as hungry as the dog.
JACK LONDON

We saw a remarkable response to kindness one time at a Bengals football game. About 25 people from our fellowship met briefly in our church parking lot, prayed, and loaded up 1,500 cold cans of pop. They set up a table near one of the entrances to the stadium and simply began asking the fans, "Would you like diet or regular? This is to show you God's love in a practical way." The workers also slipped a small business card under the top with our phone number and name. (We consider this a very soft sell, just enough to give people a point of reference if they want to look us up.)

As the evangelism team was going about this project, a Cincinnati policeman who had been directing traffic walked up. I don't know if it was his uniform, the mirrored sunglasses or his belt complete with a nightstick, but they felt intimidated and wondered what he was going to say. The policeman asked, "What are you doing?"

The team leaders responded cheerfully, "We're just giving away drinks to show God's love."

To that he asked, "Can I ask you a question? Could I have one?" Then this officer walked back to his post and carried on with directing traffic, but this time with a diet drink in his hand. To our utter surprise, he stopped some of the cars and pointed in our direction. "Do you see those people over there? They're giving away soft drinks to show God's love in a practical way."

This episode captures the essence of servant evangelism. Something in this man's heart told him, "This is an authentic group of people. They are speaking the truth." Although few words were exchanged, this policeman's heart was opened wide as we showed him love in the form of something as simple as a soft drink.

Even though this approach doesn't require a rocket scientist, it's so different from traditional programs that questions abound. We learned many lessons in consistently doing servant evangelism over the years. There are smart ways and not-so-smart ways of reaching out to our communities. In this chapter, I want to share with you several troubleshooting tips, the "nuts and bolts" of doing these kinds of projects. These simple principles helped us to effectively share the life of God with others.

PROVIDE A PLACE FOR EVERY LEVEL OF COMMITMENT

Leaders need to provide a lot of different options for becoming involved in servant evangelism. Some people can take on a large challenge, but we can expect most to only venture out occasionally. It is important to receive people at their level of readiness for doing ministry and to work with them where they actually are—not where we'd ideally like them to be.

I see people as being able to respond at four levels of commitment and challenge. A small percentage of folks are what I call the "Rambos" of evangelism because of their radical commitment and willingness to experiment in ministry. Out of more than 2,000 members in our church, I would classify about 50 as belonging in this category. These folks go out to do projects at least once every week regardless of the weather. While they don't reflect the norm, this is a good group for trying out new projects.

Not very many people can relate to the high cost of that level of outreach. We need to offer plenty of easy, entry-level projects for the bulk of believers. The more challenging projects are great and we ought not to get rid of them. The radicals thrive on the equivalent of a seven-foot high jump. On the other hand, we also need to offer a *six-inch* high jump for all those basic cowards who love Jesus. Our goal should be to provide outreach projects that can be done by the person with average gifting in evangelism.

Another group of people are the ones who go out monthly to do service projects. Still others participate in quarterly outreaches of some sort. Finally, there are a large number of people who buy in marginally to the practice of servant evangelism by doing some project on a yearly basis. I challenge people to get involved in servant evangelism about once a month. If we can get lots of people committed to going out once every four to six weeks, we will make a huge impact and no one will have to carry an undue burden. Small groups in particular seem to be able to respond to that level of frequency.

HAVE ALTERNATIVE PROJECTS SET UP IN CASE OF INCLEMENT WEATHER

I've been doing this long enough to know that Murphy's Law is real! ("Anything that can go wrong will go wrong at the worst possible moment!") While weather doesn't have to be a deterrent to our outreaches, we do need to be prepared for whatever the day may bring. Different weather just means that we will meet the needs of people in a slightly different way. If we had prepared to do a car wash and it ends up raining, we could just provide an umbrella escort at the local grocery store. If it's too cold to wash windshields, we could go door to door giving away light bulbs.

Don't lose heart in bad weather. *Do* be prepared. If you live in an area with predictably rainy weather—such as Seattle—you will need to develop a variety of rainy weather projects that reflect the needs of your community. In colder northern states and Canada, you will need to develop projects that work well with six months of snow and cold.

MINIMIZE FEARS OF PARTICIPANTS BY COMMUNICATING CLEARLY

Establish clearly defined time parameters. Clarify in advance how long you're going to be out. Making a commitment to participate in an outreach project is much easier if the time factor is made known up front. At the time of going out to do ministry, make it clear when everyone is to gather together to return home. Once you set a return time, stick to it. If you hope for quality workers to be involved with you, you'll need to be as clear as possible as to what will be expected of them each time they go out.

Make use of a "coach" in projects requiring more than 10 people. Since we used our Bible study groups and home fellowships to do most of our servant evangelism outreaches, our small-group leaders also served as the evangelism leaders for their groups. Their main job was to guarantee that each participant had an outstanding time doing the outreach project.

The coach should serve as a combination "cheerleader" (moving about to see that people are enjoying themselves) and as a "go-fer" (going for this and that). Those who make a special effort to come out and serve should never run out of the necessary supplies. The coach will need to anticipate and then resolve any problems his or her team members may encounter.

What About Getting Permission for Projects?

We seem to be living in an age of litigation madness with lawsuits being filed at the drop of a hat. Business owners are perhaps the most aware of this trend. I would recommend the following guidelines in terms of seeking permission.

1. *Ask for the minimum amount of permission for doing a project.* A Sam's warehouse store was located just down the street from our church building. We frequently visited their parking lot to do windshield washing. We never asked for permission to be on their property. We purposely started with cars in the employee parking area so that what we were doing was no secret. I suspect that if we were to actually ask permission, the official answer might have been, "No, you can't officially do that here because our insurance doesn't cover you." There isn't really a lot that can go wrong while washing windshields. Obviously, we were there to *serve*, not to sue. Don't be paranoid. If you ask enough questions, you'll find the answer is going to be no to many of your requests to do outreach projects.

2. *Don't blatantly ignore common sense regarding getting permission.* On the other hand, don't ask too many questions. It's hard to say "always" or "never" in regard to seeking permission for projects. You'll just have to be guided by your intuition. For example, if

I wanted to give away coffee inside a local mall, I would unquestionably seek permission from the mall management. However, if we were washing windshields outside in the parking lot, I might not ask for permission. At suburban grocery stores in Cincinnati, it's necessary to ask permission to give away coffee, but we regularly do this same project at an urban grocery store and never ask permission. No employee of that store has ever given us a second glance, even though we show up approximately every other Saturday morning.

3. *If you are denied permission to do a project at a promising location, offer to come back to service just the employees of that business.* I have found this a good door opener in stubborn cases. Once the managers see that you're authentic, they will likely open the door for you to come back to serve their customers. One time, we were denied permission to wash windshields at the parking lot of a nationwide department store. We felt that this would be a great locale for doing servant evangelism, so we approached the manager again and offered to do a free car wash just for the store employees. He recognized our sincere enthusiasm and invited us back.

4. *If you do encounter problems, don't forget that your smile is powerfully disarming to critics!* We rarely have any negative responses, but it is always prudent to have a strategy in case you do. Some time ago, I was washing windshields in the parking lot of a mall. An employee came out excitedly, saying, "Who do you think you are, washing windshields? You can't do

this!" My response was simply to smile. As mechanical as it may seem, a smile is a very powerful and disarming means for dealing with irate people. Then I explained what we were doing by saying, "This is a free community service project we're doing to show God's love." The employee immediately calmed down and said, "Well, if it's a community service project, I guess that's okay."

On another occasion while I was washing windshields by myself at a department store parking lot, a local rent-a-cop drove up to ask what I was doing. He had a look on his face that seemed to say, "I don't know what you're doing, but this better be good." I put on my best smile and volunteered enthusiastically, "I'm doing a free community service project to show God's love." His look of suspicion changed to a simple, "Oh." Before long, this officer was out of the car walking along with me. As I washed windshields, we talked about a variety of subjects and became virtual friends!

IF REASONABLE, RETURN TO THE SAME PLACES TO SERVE

At first, we found the management of a number of malls in the Cincinnati area where we served to be a bit skeptical. They naturally wondered what the catch was. Typically, we were granted permission with several conditions attached. After going back to those same malls for years, we gained great favor with the management. In fact, in several cases, the malls even insisted on paying for our supplies! One Christmas we were given $5,000 in wrapping paper at one mall. Another one gave us $1,500 worth of Polaroid film for a photo outreach.

*One Christmas we were given $5,000
in wrapping paper at one mall. Another one
gave us $1,500 worth of Polaroid film
for a photo outreach.*

When returning to the same locations, be sure you don't overextend your welcome. Being present too often at a particular place of business could be seen as a nuisance. In order to avoid impeding the flow of business, we made it a rule to be at a business for no more than one hour at a time. That meant that if we were going out for two hours of ministry, we generally stayed at one location for about an hour and then moved to a second locale. We wanted to avoid the appearance of "camping out" in front of any particular store. We also wanted business owners and managers to be glad to see us when we returned the next time.

WHAT SAFETY AND LIABILITY ISSUES DO WE NEED TO CONSIDER?

Here are some ideas to consider to keep you and your group members safe when you are out doing a project.

1. *Wear bright orange vests or hats if you're going to be out in traffic.* It's better to be safe than sorry if you're serving around moving vehicles. Sometimes when you do projects people get distracted by what you're doing and end up not paying close attention to their driving. Bright is better.

2. *Go in teams of a minimum of two.* Pair veterans up with newcomers and insist that people stay together. Most

of these projects are absolutely safe, but we still want to be sensitive to the fears of newcomers. Besides, it's biblical to go in pairs, and it just makes good sense. When Jesus sent out the seventy, He knew that the more experienced disciples could give faith to those who had never gone out before.

Why two instead of more? Three or more seems to be intimidating, especially if they're all men. Some projects, such as washing cars, will require a larger group. But even in these projects, I recommend using small teams of two working together in order to impart ministry skills and to promote fellowship.

3. *Use name tags for team members.* We used name tags whenever they would lend a touch of legitimacy and professionalism. Their usefulness will vary depending on your targeted areas. In a skeptical, upper-middle-class suburb, name tags can give you an extra measure of credibility. They also give you the appearance of being part of something larger than yourself. Merchants will often feel better about letting you set up a display in their store areas. If you decide to use name tags, I recommend computer-generated, professional looking ones that include the name of the church, your logo and the name of the individual who is serving.

4. *Bring cell phones.* When doing outreach projects, we usually split up into small teams within the same general area. We weren't very far from one another, but we couldn't see each other. Cell phones can be a helpful tool, especially in an urban area. Monitoring supplies and dealing with questions becomes much easier

without having to track people down. Remember, one of the primary goals of each outing is to make sure each participant has a positive experience and leaves wanting to come back for the next one.

WHAT EQUIPMENT CONCERNS SHOULD WE CONSIDER?

Keep the following points in mind when you or your group members are purchasing equipment or using equipment out on a project.

1. *Use high-quality equipment.* The people you are serving will feel valued if you use high quality products. Conversely, the impact of your service can be compromised if you use inferior equipment. Often the difference between mediocre and excellent requires just a little bit more money and a little bit more effort.

2. *Learn to use your equipment properly.* None of the projects we commonly did required an extreme measure of expertise, but some insightful training was needed in most. I always spent a few minutes covering the bases regarding each project before we set out. For example, washing windshields isn't very difficult, but if you aren't familiar with a squeegee, you can easily streak the window. A well-cleaned windshield will be noticed by the driver. On the other hand, a streaked windshield is irritating and even worse than a dirty one. Before going out, newcomers need a short lesson on avoiding streaks.

   Certain projects make speed and efficiency more important. For example, the sheer number of cars pulling into a free car wash often creates a traffic jam. We need to do a superior job of serving people in our projects without adding extra hassle to their busy lives. The time spent in training and organization will increase the speed and quality in our services.

3. *Over-purchase supplies.* It is better to have leftover supplies than to run out when you're in the midst of an outreach. By running out of equipment or supplies, you're making a very negative statement to your workers: "We weren't expecting anything great to happen here today." A good rule of thumb is to have enough for that outreach plus the next one. You'll use the extras soon enough. Most of the supplies needed for projects you will do are inexpensive, so over-purchasing is typically more a matter of planning than finances.

4. *Establish an equipment closet.* There's no need to reinvent the wheel every time you go out to do servant evangelism. I know of nothing more irritating in doing projects than getting people gathered, sensing the Lord's presence and blessing, only to find a glitch in the area of equipment. I believe that it's important to have an ample supply of whatever you may need for a particular type of ministry.

Our closet consisted of brooms, rakes, window squeegees, cases of soft drinks, ice chests, toilet cleaning kits, car washing equipment, light bulbs, batteries for smoke detectors, leaf blowers, and so forth. I wanted to create an atmosphere for those who gathered to serve that we were equipped for come what may. I also wanted them to know that we could take on as many workers as showed up. My hope was that those who went to do ministry one week would feel enthusiastic enough to bring their friends the next week.

BE SURE TO DO A QUALITY JOB

These free deeds of love make a powerful impression on those we serve—but only if we do a good job. The media often portrays Christians as being out of touch with fashion and current trends, and doing just enough to get by in life. This image is untrue and unfair, but we need to reckon with it just the same. If we do a bang-up, quality job, then we will go a long way toward tearing down these negative images.

We don't need to be neurotic perfectionists, but a reasonably good job is within reach of everyone.

If you are taking a role of leadership in servant evangelism projects, I recommend *The E Myth* by Michael Gerber. This book discusses the difficulty in maintaining quality services as projects and businesses grow. Both churches and businesses are often victims of their own success. Our initial success can yield more participants but can also diminish the level of quality. We don't need to be neurotic perfectionists, but a reasonably good job is within reach of everyone.

Every once in a while we would get a phone call from a dissatisfied customer complaining that we did more harm than good in our attempt to serve. One time, someone complained that we smeared the window of his recently washed car. In cases like that, we always offered to pay for a professional car wash. We were not discouraged by phone calls from irate people; instead, we just decided to do a better job on our next outing.

ALLOW TIME AFTER A PROJECT FOR PARTICIPANTS TO DOWNLOAD

I have found it helpful to have a debriefing time in the wake of ministry. I refer to this as a "do and tell" time—now that we've done something, let's talk about it, compare notes and let our hair down. This gives people the chance to bring to completion the process of learning. They truly learn what they can do, digest (information) and discuss. Jesus apparently did something similar when He received back the seventy after they had gone out to minister God's love to the surrounding towns and villages. They returned from their missions and shared lots of stories with one another.

For our projects, we began with *words* of training. We then did *works* of training as we put the theory into practice. And then we compared accounts with others who had stepped out along with us to give away God's life. Spirited discussions often followed ministry outings. After we would go out, we usually gathered at a fast-food restaurant at a designated time. Over a taco and burrito, the conversation may sound something like this: "How did it go with you?" "When you served people, did they seem open?" "Which project did you enjoy the most?" "What did you say or do differently that could help us to be more effective the next time we go out?" "Where shall we go next time?"

Beginning anything new is a lot easier when we have a "loose grip" attitude. This is best achieved when our primary goal is to enjoy ourselves and just have fun with one another. Evangelism then becomes a byproduct of our fun. A newcomer to servant evangelism once confided in me, "You know, you can't pay to have this much fun in the world."

RECORD WHAT YOU'VE LEARNED FOR FUTURE REFERENCE

Any energy spent in recording what you've learned after each outing will be well spent. Each time you'll gain insight into how to more effectively give away God's love. Notice what words seem to hit home, what products work the best, and how much of each product to bring along. Take note of which shopping areas are the most receptive to your outreach gestures and return there. You will notice a marked difference in the atmosphere and receptivity of certain stores and neighborhoods. Some are definitely more friendly and responsive than others.

Also, keep a log of how many people you are touching with various amounts of goods and services. Keeping a record of numbers can be helpful for both personal motivation and practical purposes, like supply needs. Knowing trends can also help leaders to evaluate and plan for future growth.

DON'T BE CONCERNED WITH THE IMMEDIATE RETURN OF YOUR EFFORTS

Resist the temptation to take your results too seriously. For every person we served, our experience has shown that two or three more were indirectly touched. Those we contacted typically went on to tell others, "You wouldn't believe what just happened to me." One time, we hosted a team of teenagers who did outreach for several weeks during the summer. These teens received basic training in a variety of ministry skills and then spent their afternoons going out into the community to do various outreach projects.

> *I believe that much of the time we see only the tip of the iceberg of how our serving affects others.*

At the end of their second week, the teens were in need of a little pep talk to lift their spirits. Cincinnati's hot and humid summers can wear anyone down. We estimated that they had *directly* served 6,000 people and *indirectly* touched another group of at least equal size by shock value alone. That meant that we had communicated God's love to 12,000 people over the two-week period.

I believe that much of the time we see only the tip of the iceberg of how our serving affects others. Probably the best stories remain unknown to us. My guess is that we'll hear some of the conclusions to our projects when we get to heaven. I expect to meet a few folks who walk up and identify themselves as "I'm the guy you gave a cup of coffee to in downtown Cincinnati one time. That was the beginning of my coming to know Christ."

On a Friday afternoon when we were giving away cold drinks, a young man named Josh met an older woman as she came up to the stoplight. She said, "The last time you gave me a drink I cried all the way home. I realized that God loves me."

Josh quickly replied, "Well I guess you're gonna cry all the way home today, too. Here's your drink!"

Pray Before, Pray During and Pray After

Intercede for your projects. Remember, servant evangelism involves "low-risk/high-grace" projects. It is very easy to underestimate the spiritual side of what is going on in people's hearts. We must remember that we are absolutely dependent upon the Lord's presence for fruitfulness. If God is upon these deeds of service, then those we touch will be drawn toward

Christ. If the Holy Spirit isn't upon these works, then they aren't much more than nice but empty gestures.

Our attitude must be, "If God shows up, something wonderful is going to happen here. If He doesn't, then we won't see much impact." Jesus tells us that His will is for us to bear fruit that will remain (see John 15:16). Our fruit will remain as we depend on the presence and blessing of God for success in outreach projects.

Pray as you serve. As we are conducting these projects, our prayers should be simple, perhaps along these lines: "Come, Holy Spirit. Anoint this project. Use these simple acts of love to broadcast Your reality and love to every single person we encounter today. Let them forget us, but remember You."

Pray as you finish. When you finish your outreach project, I recommend that you spend a few moments in prayer sealing your efforts before God. Tell the Lord that you are dependent upon Him for lasting influence to occur in the lives you've touched. Ask the Holy Spirit to follow the people you've touched all the way home. Invite Him to have His way in their lives.

If you find yourself with someone who wants prayer, don't embarrass the person by doing something outlandish. . . . Be sensitive to where most people you'll encounter are spiritually.

What about praying for people while doing serving projects? You will be amazed at how many people are actually open to receiving prayer in public. It isn't always appropriate to pray—or even to offer to pray—for those we are serving. Sometimes though, it just fits. Our rule of thumb is this: *Be open to praying for people if they seem open to it.* We want them to invite us into their lives. We aren't coming on like gangbusters knocking down the door to their hearts.

If you find yourself with someone who wants prayer, don't embarrass the person by doing something outlandish. Although you may be comfortable praying out loud or loudly, be sensitive to where most people are spiritually. Don't lay hands on them; they won't understand. Also, it's absolutely fine to pray a short prayer with your eyes open. When we prayed for folks, we usually asked them to contact us to let us know what happened in response to the prayer offered. Our hope was that people would begin to look for God's action in their lives as further evidence of His love for them.

A DELAYED REACTION

Jesus saw it as imperative that we conduct ourselves in the power of the love of God. His love flowing through our lives is the imprimatur of our King, signifying that we are followers of the one true God. The human heart is designed by the Creator to respond to the presence of love. Paul refers to this built-in sensitivity when he writes, "The creation eagerly waits for the revealing of the sons of God" (Rom. 8:19). Even in its darkened and fallen spiritual state, the world is intuitively looking for the "sons of God."

Once when we were giving out food just before Christmas, we met a woman who confided in us that both she and her husband were unemployed. We gave her food and then offered to pray for her. She received prayer from us although she openly questioned the concept of a benevolent God in light of her recent difficulties.

After we prayed we didn't have any further contact with this woman until almost a year later. Then a few weeks before that next Christmas, she called to tell us that she had finally found a great new job, just what she'd wanted. She was so grateful for what had happened in her life the year before that she wanted to take in donations from the other employees and then give us the money to purchase more food for the needy. Our part in that wonderful answer to prayer was small, but just hearing the results of our little seed was very encouraging.

Proverbs 11:30 promises us that "he who wins souls is wise." You and I will have plenty of job security as we step out to lead others to Christ. There are lots of souls who need winning, each one suffering significant pain in many areas of life. As we touch those pains, we will be able to impart a message of hope for a future in Jesus Christ.

One group of students I know offers a tutoring service for struggling underclassmen. It seems only natural to conclude their sessions with a little prayer asking God's help for the upcoming exam. After doing this for many years, these godly tutors have received many encouraging stories from students who have seen miracles on their tests. Such positive results provide open doors for further conversations about the God who gives us grace and wisdom in abundance.

More Kindness

Live in anticipation of the opportunity to give to others. Look for opportunities. Walk through the door before you!

Each week, I purchase a case of inexpensive products such as chewing gum or breath mints. I carry 10 packs or so of several different varieties in my pocket, and offer them to whomever I meet. I don't ask, "Would you like some gum?" Instead I offer by saying, "Which would you prefer?"

In the checkout lines at most retail stores, there are soft drinks available for spontaneous purchase, which I usually do—for those around me. I never ask, "Would you like a soft drink?" I've made that mistake, and was turned down each time. Now

I'm never turned down. I say, "So are you a diet or regular Coke/Pepsi person?" (Don't be shy—jump right in there!) No one has ever ignored me, and I have done this all over the U.S. and in major cities around the world. I normally end up buying three or four drinks. I pay for them and then hand them out, saying something like, "I just think it's better to show God's love than to talk about God's love . . ." I usually give each person a connect card. Often the people huddle together, read the card together and talk.

CHAPTER 8

Children Are Naturals

There must be more to life than having everything!
MAURICE SENDAK

Most families are under increasing time pressures. Statistics show the average American enjoys 17 percent less leisure time now than just 10 years ago. In spite of the hectic pace of life, my wife and I always made it a priority to take our children out to do service projects twice a month. Janie and I believed that they would be receiving an incomplete spiritual education if they only read Bible stories and spent time in Sunday School. Our children needed to learn that getting outside the four walls of the church to interact with the lost and the poor was a normal part of the Christian life.

We took our children along on church buses that had been especially designed for ministry to the poor. We had the seats removed and replaced with racks for food and clothing so that each bus was capable of hauling 150 bags of groceries and enough clothes to outfit a small army. Once we loaded up, we drove to various parts of Cincinnati where we could find a concentration of folks in need. Since the poor often lack transportation to reach sources of help, we remedied this by simply going to them! Once we arrived, we turned on some contemporary Christian music and began to invite the neighborhood out for free food and clothes.

When my daughter Laura was eight years old, she agreed to go with me on one of these trips. However, when Saturday morning rolled around, she had become engrossed in watching cartoons. After a little persuasion, we reached a compromise: I bribed my daughter by agreeing to take her to McDonald's later if she went. I was amazed how quickly she was dressed and buckled into the waiting car!

After we arrived at an inner-city housing project, we began to help people carry bags of groceries from the bus to their apartments. A couple of young mothers got off the bus with their arms overflowing with groceries and clothes. As we walked along chatting with these women, I received a word of knowledge. I "saw" in my mind's eye a picture of a knee with a red light blinking on its left side. I asked the lady if she had a knee problem. She said she did. In the next moment several more specific bits of information came to me. Somehow I knew that she had slipped on a patch of ice in front of her apartment in January. I also knew that her doctor had told her that she would probably need surgery, a prospect that made her fearful.

Laura saw that God uses imperfect people— even her parents! Most of all, she experienced the power of God moving through her very normal, eight-year-old frame.

The woman was flabbergasted as I shared this with her. She said, "I know who you are—a man of God!" She was not just open to our praying for her, but she was also enthusiastic! I had Laura place her hand on the woman's knee and coached her in praying for the power of God to remove the pain and damaged tissue. To Laura's amazement, she saw the presence of the Lord come upon her. The damaged knee became warm and the part that had been hurting felt numb to the woman.

I was excited about God's work of healing, but wanted to share this as more of a *perspective* story than a *power* story. Laura experienced something very powerful that morning that might easily stick with her the rest of her life. She saw God touch a woman in a dynamic way. She saw that God uses imperfect people—even her parents! Most of all, she experienced the power of God moving through her very normal, eight-year-old frame.

The Church of today needs a new perspective on the role of children in ministering to the needs of others. They are capable of being used powerfully. The boy Samuel proved that he could hear God's call, accurately discern God's will, and even prophesy regarding the future. Too often children have been seen only as the *future* Church, when in reality they are a vital part of the Church today, whatever their age. Unless we can give these little ones a more important role in outreach, we will miss the opportunity of having some of our best evangelists touch the world. For their own sake, our children need to grow up in a home built not on a theory of Christianity but on the ongoing expression of God's love and grace to others.

CHILDREN—OUR BEST EVANGELISTS

On Palm Sunday, Jesus admonished the Jewish leaders that if the people were quiet the very rocks would cry out in praise (see Luke 19:29-40). I have sometimes wondered why the Lord *didn't* use rocks. They are plentiful, obedient and always ready. People, on the other hand, are fickle and undependable. Young children are a lot like rocks. They are plentiful, usually obedient and consistently more available than adults. Unlike adults, children don't set so many conditions on their obedience.

It's possible that children are the Church's best evangelists. Consider that possibility with me.

Children Are Available

One of the most powerful miracles in the Gospels comes through the obedience, purity and innocence of a little boy. After Jesus had been teaching for a couple of days, the crowd of several thousand people had grown hungry. Since the town was too distant, the apostles went through the crowd, asking, "Who has food they can share?"

The bad news for the apostles was that only a small bit of food was available—just the lunch of a young boy. I believe others probably had food, but none of the adults were willing to share. They rationalized their way out of offering their own meager sustenance. For practical purposes, the only food available was the lunch prepared by the boy's mother, some loaves and fish.

Jesus didn't seem concerned. After giving thanks for what God had made available, he directed the apostles to distribute food to those gathered on the hillside. I believe that little lunch didn't suddenly turn into a gigantic mound of bread and fish, but kept appearing bit by bit as the disciples began to hand it out. Jesus makes it clear that a little, combined with the presence of God, adds up to plenty for even a crowd of thousands to eat more than their fill.

During the busy summer season, many people find it difficult to maintain their lawns, so we would often load several lawn mowers into trucks and drive about the neighborhoods of Cincinnati looking for long grass. It was really easy for our lawn crews to spot those who needed ministry. As we drove up to one house, we could hear the sound of the Reds baseball game filtering through the screen door. Our team leader knocked on the door and explained what we wanted to do. A man sat emotionless in an Archie Bunker-style easy chair—in front of the tube with beer in hand. His only response was, "Sure, go ahead and cut my grass. Whatever." We were surprised he didn't react to our unusual offer. How often does someone stop by and offer to cut your grass for free?

The team made quick work of the unkempt lawn. Within 30 minutes we had cut, edged and bagged all the grass. The leader knocked at the door to tell the man that we had done this to show him God's love in a way he could understand. His response was again fairly unemotional, "Okay. Thanks."

As they walked down the porch steps, 10-year-old Adam told his dad the Lord had given him a word of knowledge. We trained the children of our church to see it as natural to receive such words from the Lord when He wanted to touch someone. We also incorporated praying for the sick into our regular Sunday School curriculum. Adam's words of knowledge had proven to be accurate on several other occasions, so the adults on this particular outing took him seriously.

Adam sensed that the Lord wanted us to pray for this man that his pain be relieved. We didn't know what his pain was, but we cautiously went forward to take advantage of this apparent opportunity. After mowing the lawn the team felt they had enough of a connection to step out in boldness and say, "Before leaving we want to just pray for you briefly."

The man reluctantly agreed. Since Adam had gotten the word, it was only appropriate that he should pray. As they stood in a circle, the boy offered a prayer that was simple and to the point: "Lord, come now and relieve the pain in this man's heart."

What followed next amazed even these veteran servant evangelists. The man began to sob uncontrollably! After a few minutes he had thoroughly wet the shoulder of the person nearest him. After his emotions calmed down, the man explained that his wife had been hospitalized for surgery. His 19-year-old son had been caught just the previous night stealing a car to support his drug habit. This man had been sitting in his living room that morning feeling absolutely overwhelmed by these family troubles.

This story highlights some of the advantages children have over more sophisticated adult believers. The grown-up team members placed a premium on time and were ready to go on to the next house. Because this child wasn't in any hurry at all, he was able to realize that the purposes of God were not yet fulfilled. Adults tend to be fearful of looking bad in public, so they were slow to suggest praying for a stranger. Without Adam's simple prayer, perhaps this man's heart would not have been unlocked to receive God's comfort.

Adam has no problem believing that God is real, and that God wants to use him to influence the world.

Just as important was what happened to Adam himself. I have spoken to his parents several times about that day. They believe that something significant was planted in Adam's heart when he saw the man radically touched as a fruit of his prayer. While children learn by what they are told, they are always more likely to remember what they experience. This young boy has no problem believing that God is real, *and* that God wants to use him to influence the world. Many adult believers don't really believe that God wants to use them or even could use them if they made themselves available.

Children Have Credibility

Several years ago, I saw something regarding children in ministry that was odd yet enlightening. One of the course requirements for a Bible college class on the cults was to attend a meeting of the

Jehovah's Witnesses at the local Kingdom Hall. Having never been to a meeting of a cultic group, I found the evening intimidating and was glad that a couple of friends came along as moral support.

The meeting consisted mainly of leaders doing a little bit of Bible teaching and mostly exhorting the people to get out and evangelize more. At several points in the evening, they practiced their witnessing skills by role-playing with others in the group. One aspect of their meetings that I found very interesting was their use of children to do evangelism. Though their belief system is riddled with unbiblical perceptions of God and life, I had to admire their insight for letting children open doors to people's hearts. These young Jehovah's Witnesses resembled little robots, spouting off memorized party lines of church doctrines. The leaders knew that while most people wouldn't hesitate to slam the door on an adult door-knocker, the public is probably not going to be rude to a child.

Children are disarming. While we never want to *use* children, they do cause outsiders to take notice of God. Inside every adult, just beneath the skin, is a child who has some idea of God. Children serve as a reminder of the simplicity of our relationship with God. When they tell someone, "We're serving you to show you God's love," adults listen.

I never like to see children spouting off spiritual truth that is not real to them. In fact, they don't need to say much. Children effectively model God's love simply by being children. By their simplicity and trust, they depict the clearest picture of a lifestyle that is obedient to the Lord Jesus. Perhaps it was for these qualities that Jesus said we must become as little children to enter the kingdom of God (see Matt. 18:3).

Children Are the Doorway into the Church for Outsiders
When children speak (or cry), it seems people really listen. My wife, Janie, and I noticed this when our first child was just a few

months old. We were amazed to see that just about everybody loves babies. We would go into restaurants and complete strangers would smile and begin to talk to us about their children or grandchildren. Before long we would naturally get into other topics, often talking about God. It seems that the presence of children inclines our thoughts toward God. For example, when children come along in their marriage, many baby boomers who may have avoided organized religion seek out a church home.

I once met a woman in her mid-seventies at a newcomers' coffee. I naturally asked how she happened to come to our church. She told me a heartwarming story. This woman was housebound for several months after her back was broken in an accident. One Sunday morning, she was lying on the couch watching a TV preacher and wishing she were well enough to go to church. Just then her doorbell rang. Standing on her porch were a couple of boys with an adult supervisor and a marigold plant.

These two boys were part of a class that trained children in areas such as ministry to the poor, praying for the sick and being members of "God's Secret Service" (servant evangelism boiled down to a child's level). We offered these classes during the summers as an alternative to our normal Sunday School program. Our goal was to provide opportunities where children could actually *see* the working of God.

When this woman opened her door, they explained, "We're giving out plants this morning to show God's love to you in a practical way." She was so touched by the gesture that she cried even in retelling the story months afterward. When she got better she decided to find out what kind of Christians would give away flowers to show God's love. She came and decided to join.

Children Are Fearless!
Researchers report that all of us are born with just a handful of natural fears that are oriented to self-preservation. Out of those

basic survival instincts, less healthy fears crop up. As we get older, living in fear becomes for many of us a way of life. Unless we learn how to deal with our fears, we often become even more cautious as we grow older.

Most adults are reticent to do any sort of outreach because they fear failure. We've been conditioned to think that failure is a painful thing that ought to be avoided. The truth is that failure is the necessary doorway to growing and learning about most things in life. Children haven't been conditioned to play it safe. Most of them are free from the fears that plague and even paralyze adults.

For example, how many adults do you know who would be willing to sell candy at the neighborhood grocery store? It seems that every time I go shopping at the local supermarket, I see children from soccer leagues or Little League or Girl Scouts selling candy by the exit. I'm a sucker for kids selling things, so I always buy something even though I don't like candy!

One church I know of in the New York City area doesn't allow fear of danger to hinder their evangelistic efforts. With adult oversight, a small army of children goes out into the neighborhood in a variety of creative ways. They regularly touch 400 to 500 people within a couple of hours through free face painting, helium balloons, Polaroid photos and cold drinks. In that setting it is only natural for these young evangelists to tell the neighborhood children about Christ. The parents have been so impressed by such friendliness that many new families have been added to the church.

BENEFITS TO CHILDREN WHEN THEY DO SERVANT EVANGELISM

Some enormous benefits come to the children whose families regularly reach out to serve their communities through these kinds of projects. Let's consider a few of these growth points.

Children Become Outward in an Age of Introversion

The electronic age has shaped our lives toward inwardness. By adolescence, the average child has become well acquainted with cable TV, take-out food, video games, cell phones, computers, the Internet, iPods and DVDs. Although these conveniences can serve a useful purpose, they also encourage us to spend a significant amount of time by ourselves. Many of us spend too much time alone, creating an ever-shrinking circle of relationships.

In her book *The Popcorn Report*, futurist Faith Popcorn calls this increasing trend in America "cocooning," digging into our "high-tech caves" as a way to remain safe from the intimidating world about us. Popcorn projects that it will soon be possible to hole up for weeks, maybe even months, at a time without leaving the security of our homes.[1]

The Christian community is no stranger to this phenomenon of cocooning. I once spoke with a man who attended Christian schools from nursery school through graduate school. At the end of nearly two decades of being sheltered, he discovered that he had been poorly prepared for life in the real world. After coming out of his spiritual funk, this man confided in me that he wanted to develop a new, realistic Christian life that included those who don't yet know Jesus Christ. Servant evangelism provides a practical way to encourage this outward directedness at a younger age.

Children Become Sensitive to the Moving of the Holy Spirit

Youngsters seem to feel at home with the idea that God can work through them, but this natural sensitivity is soon lost if it remains untapped. The best way for children to grow in their awareness of the Holy Spirit's action is through firsthand experience. The presence of the Lord is not an idea to be mastered in the context of a book but a heart knowledge that becomes real as we minister to others. Serving large numbers of people convinces our children (and us) that something unique is happening with each person we touch.

The presence of the Lord is not an idea to be mastered in the context of a book, but a heart knowledge that becomes real as we minister to others.

Something wells up in people as they see the Spirit moving in clear ways upon others. Jesus tells us that "the eye is the lamp of the body" (Matt. 6:22, *RSV*). What we see through our "lamps" is taken into our hearts. When children see people being healed and empowered through the gifts of the Holy Spirit, they themselves become hungry to be touched and used by God. When children see God move, I believe that something is planted *inside* of them that will last a lifetime.

Children Look to Their Parents to Model Christianity
One popular television show is *The Simpsons*, a sitcom that pokes fun at parent-child relationships. Like any caricature, the humor merely exaggerates the reality of typical family life. Children certainly have plenty of opportunities to see the weaknesses and shortcomings of their parents. As parents, we need to continually find new ways of showing the life of the Lord to our children.

Scripture promises us that if we "train up a child in the way he should go . . . when he is old he will not depart from it" (Prov. 22:6). That training goes far beyond imparting information. We must show them Jesus, the Son of God who is the way, the truth, and the life. Children learn and grow by doing, not just by hearing Bible stories and doing "sword" drills. Authentic change happens from the inside out. We need to model for our children how the life of God changes us as agents of His grace going out into our communities.

It is vital that children see their parents express their beliefs in clear ways, both by word and deed. Experts tell us that only about 10 percent of our communication is done verbally. We constantly model our attitudes through our behavior. Our children will pay a lot more attention to what we do than to what we say. Children must see that following Jesus Christ involves *obeying* the will of God as well as *learning* the will of God. They need to have parents who not only *know* the truth but also live the truth of God.

As parents, we must regularly ask ourselves, *What sort of Christianity am I living out before my children? Do I reflect a healthy balance between receiving and giving the life of God, or do I resemble the Dead Sea that takes in much but gives off little and grows saltier year by year?* The brand of Christianity our children adopt will probably look a lot like that which we have demonstrated, despite the correct Christian words we may have spoken along the way.

How to Take Your Family into the Community

We are living in an age of unbelievable rebellion and confusion, a time when children can even go to court and divorce their parents. Increasingly, negative news edges out the few positive reports on the horizon. As society becomes more and more dangerous, especially for children, our natural response is to run away and hide. The church serves many believers as primarily a secure shelter *from* the world. A more biblical response is to run wisely into the world.

We are called to let the light of Christ pierce the surrounding darkness. Invading this darkness isn't as impossible as it may seem. Here are some tips I've discovered in bringing light into the darkness with my family.

Start with a Simple, "Safe" Project

A primary goal in taking your children out to do service projects is to provide positive experiences with evangelism. We want to build up their courage, which can overflow into more advanced areas of ministry later on. All of the servant evangelism projects listed in appendix 1 are generally nonthreatening. Go with the ones that appeal to you.

One consideration is the age and abilities of your children. For example, it would probably not be a good idea to take small children out washing windshields because they aren't tall enough to reach. Even older children are likely to streak the windows because they often don't have a well developed eye for detail. Another case of project incompatibility with children occurs every time we conduct a car wash. Without fail, a small child will want to hold one of the hoses. That is not a good idea. Most kids lack enough skill or good judgment when it comes to controlling a running hose. When everyone gets wet, including the people we're trying to serve, we end up leaving a poor impression.

A more manageable car wash alternative would be to have children wash the wheels or the bumpers. Another easy and sure-fire project involves distributing drinks in front of a grocery store on a Saturday morning. Plugging parking meters is also a favorite for children who are tall enough. Meanwhile, an adult could slip a little flyer under the windshield wiper.

For the past several summers, several dozen churches around the country have sponsored a program called Summer of Service, or S.O.S. In this program, young people from high school or college who are considering the ministry as a profession are given a safe and positive experience with different sorts of outreach. Many of these students are petrified at the thought of going out to the community with God's love. After just a few days of serving, a significant breakthrough frequently occurs. Once they've gotten a positive evangelism experience under their belt, they more easily assume greater degrees of risk in ministry.

Be *Wise*—Supervise!

Without question we live in dangerous times, but children can learn valuable lessons for life by getting out into the real world under proper supervision. It is imperative that we proceed with wisdom when doing service projects. Before we even go out, we discuss with the children some of the realities of the world in which we live. We are coming with the mercy and compassion of God, but because of the state of the world, some of those we serve are hurting and even seriously disturbed. Some safety guidelines we follow on ministry outings with children include the following:

- *All ministry is conducted with adults.* This principle is especially important for children. Some places you will visit may be unsavory. You don't necessarily need to avoid going to those places; you just need to go at certain times of the day when you will feel safe. Always go with plenty of adult supervision.

- *Children must always stay with adult supervisors.* Children can talk to strangers, but only in the presence of adult leaders. We always told the children who went with us on our projects that they were never to leave the area where the service project was taking place. In providing a positive experience, we allowed the children to do most of the ministry, with the adults looking over their shoulder. Depending on the project and the age of the children, we kept things manageable by having at least one adult for every three children.

Go Out with Your Children *Regularly*

I recommend that you plan several ministry outings in advance or else you'll find yourself going out only once in a great while. Ideally, I'd shoot for going out once per month. Saturday morning works well for many families. I recommend that you not attempt projects that require longer than two hours. The goal here is to quit before it feels like drudgery to your children. It's better to leave them having fun instead of driving the project into the ground. With younger children who have even shorter attention spans, you will need to plan accordingly.

The goal is to quit before it feels like drudgery to your children. It's better to leave them having fun instead of driving the project into the ground.

After Going Out, Spend Time *Downloading*

Go out after your project for a burger and a time of sharing. This is an ideal time to get feedback from the child's perspective. While it's still fresh in their minds, ask them to share any victories, insights, or fears they felt while serving. Children need help interpreting their ministry experiences. Remember, you are building lasting memories that will help to mold their views about God, life, and your own Christianity.

Seek to Make Ministry *Fun*!

Over the years, we coined an expression that is *almost* straight from Scripture: "Where the Spirit of the Lord is, there is fun!"

More than anything else, the best guarantee for influencing your children with the kingdom of God is to make your ministry time fun! The only activities any of us do long-term are those we enjoy. Children are especially motivated to seek fun. With ministry I've seen that if I'm not having fun, neither will my children.

If children observe their parents serving out of duty or sheer commitment, they will get a bad taste in their mouths for church, ministry, and perhaps even for God. I am convinced that duty-oriented Christianity has turned many more children off to the Lord than any recognized enemy of the faith, such as secular humanism. If you present an attractive and enjoyable picture of what it means to be a Christian, they are more likely to see it as something they can commit themselves to for life. And most importantly, they will build a picture of a God that is positive and approachable.

One tool we used is to hold a monthly "Matthew's Party." This is a takeoff on the party recorded in Luke 5 where Matthew throws a celebration to mark his conversion to following Jesus as the Messiah. In his joy, Matthew invited his friends who had never met Jesus to have dinner with the Lord. We would also sponsor a party in a particular neighborhood and invite everyone to have dinner with the Lord and us.

At one Matthew's Party, we drew more than 1,000 guests from an inner-city neighborhood. We hung a 20-foot-wide banner that read, "It's Party Time!" We fired up our grill on wheels that could roast 300 hot dogs at a time. We put on loud music and called the neighborhood out to have fun with us. Basically, we took over the better part of the park adjoining a low-income housing project. Entire families from our church attended because this outreach involved some sort of ministry for every adult and child.

As I looked around, it was heartwarming to see so much practical love being shared with a hurting neighborhood. One group was fixing and cleaning a swing set. Another cluster of folks was clipping weeds and sweeping up broken glass. Others were leading organized games for the neighborhood children. About 20 adults and children dressed up as clowns and did silly stuff. Still another group was tossing frisbees around the park with kids from the housing projects. Positive bonds were being formed everywhere around the party.

"Thanks for putting this on. There is something almost tangible of the Lord's presence here. You can almost feel Him here in the park. I know this is making a powerful impact on my son. Today he has seen and felt what I've been telling him about God all his life."

One of the parents from our church came up to me in the midst of all this activity and said, "Thanks for putting this on. There is something almost tangible of the Lord's presence here. You can almost feel Him here in the park. I know this is making a powerful impact on my son. Today he has seen and felt what I've been telling him about God all his life."

Jesus wants all of us to head toward matching our works with our words. To do so, we're going to need new leaders who are free from the fears that have held back so many believers. What more appropriate group from whom to learn boldness than our children.

MORE KINDNESS

Fifteen years after I wrote *Conspiracy of Kindness*, this chapter about bringing children and youth onto the scene is the one I feel even more strongly about.

I plead with you: Whatever your children's ages, do whatever it takes to see them become integrally involved with outward-focused ministries. If you catch on to this simple message and put it into practice, I believe that you and I will talk one day in heaven and that you will thank me immensely for being so insistent.

At the time I was writing *Conspiracy of Kindness*, my children were at home, in school and growing up. As a parent, I now realize that growing up takes many decades. When children move out, there are many more phases of parenting yet to come. When children move on, get into careers and begin to make decisions on their own, then it becomes clearer what kind of person you have raised.

Living out the serving lifestyle was something Janie and I tried to model for our kids each day—for decades—and we are thrilled that they see serving as an engaging and fun way to live life! At the time of this writing, my two older daughters are in their mid- to late-20s and have begun their careers. My son, Jack, is just finishing high school. Every day or two, one of my children calls me to share a story about something amazing that happened as they stepped out to serve someone. Nearly all of their friends have become believers after a few months to a year. That hasn't happened because our children are eager-beaver evangelists; they simply treat their friends with dignity, respect and practical love.

To set that cycle in motion doesn't take long to activate, and it will always bear fruit—lasting fruit. It turns out the Reformer Martin Luther was right all along: It is not the responsibility of the Church to impart a spiritual foundation to our children. When the yogurt hits the fan with our children—as it inevitably will with each of them—it is absolutely inappropriate for parents to blame the Church or youth leaders. If any anger is due, the finger is best pointed at ourselves.

We are parents living lives that our children will pick up on
and mimic as they grow old and enter into adulthood.

Note

1. Faith Popcorn, *The Popcorn Report* (New York: Doubleday Currency, 1991), p. 27.

Small Groups Turned Inside Out

It is one of the most beautiful compensations of life that no man can sincerely try to help another without helping himself.
RALPH WALDO EMERSON

When my church was still small, we started meeting together in support groups made up of five or so members. My group consisted of a machinist, a female karate instructor (a black belt), a receptionist, a sales agent, and a homemaker. We had little in common outside of our relationship with Jesus Christ, but that glue was strong enough to bind us together in love.

Most churches include several groups that meet for a variety of purposes. These smaller clusters offer support on a more personal level as well as an opportunity to develop deeper relationships. Most groups, if left to themselves, will grow cozy and closed. Newcomers are often tolerated rather than heartily welcomed and find it difficult to break in. One of the best ways to avoid ingrown groups is to have them practice servant evangelism together.

On the second night in a new group, we began discussing a plan for outreach. One spontaneous person said, "Why don't we go out right now! We'll pack some bags of food and be on our way." I myself am typically more calculated in my approach to ministry, but a groupthink dynamic seized everyone and before I could add a word of caution we were on our way! We decided to give away food in a nearby housing area where many needy families lived. We went to the store, bought some generic food, and packed our bags into a station wagon. Then our group split into twos and decided to reconvene an hour later.

A groupthink dynamic seized everyone and before I could add a word of caution we were on our way!

Our approach was simple: We would knock on doors, offer food and ask if we could pray for any needs. My partner and I gave away four bags of food to several families. Twice we met families who said, "We could use some food, but so-and-so is *really* in need of food. Why don't you give it to them and if you have any left over come back here." Another single mom we met said she not only needed food but was wondering what it meant to be a Christian. After a short explanation of the gospel, we were able to pray with her to invite Jesus Christ into her heart.

The hour of designated time seemed to fly by, as if we had entered some kind of time warp. We gathered back together to share stories of our personal encounters. Some of them seemed almost unbelievable. One other team had prayed with someone to accept Jesus as Savior. Another had run into a family that had been out of food for a couple of days and weren't scheduled to receive food stamps for another week.

Still another pair had met a woman whose arm was para-lyzed from a recent stroke. They had prayed a simple prayer, "Come, Lord, and heal this woman's arm." If they hadn't brought her with them, I wouldn't have believed the amazing results. In front of me stood a grandmotherly woman who enthusiastically reported to me that she had felt an instant, mild, electrical shock flow through her shoulder and arm to her fingertips. Feeling in her arm and even mobility in her fingers returned.

We were all stunned. What we saw is the stuff the book of Acts is written about. Several years later, that evening still stands out as one of the most spectacular of my life. We saw for the first time that God works in wonderful ways through common believers who step out to do the ministry of Jesus in our neighborhoods. I had prayed for the sick before and I had given out plenty of bags of groceries. Frankly, something good happened in most of my attempts at outreach, but most of the time I had operated as a "Lone Ranger."

I realized through this experience that God *really* likes to move through a group that steps out to serve the needs of others. Groups proved to be the greenhouse that allowed the life of the Holy Spirit to flourish in our midst. Our church went on to include more than 200 small groups—ranging from those focused on fellowship to Bible studies, women's groups, men's groups, recovery groups or "affinity" groups who gather around a common interest such as bicycling, fishing or a creative craft of some sort.

Your church probably has many groups already in place—such as a choir, a women's circle, or various boards and committees—each of which has a distinct identity and focus. Each group could be a closed circle that exists to itself alone, or it could be a bridge that takes the life of God out into the community. Try an experiment: Cut your meeting time in half and go out to wash windshields. I predict that your group will develop a new level of intimacy as a result of this shared task. As groups cultivate a value for reaching out beyond themselves, they are much more likely to survive and to create an atmosphere of healing for its members.

A LIGHTHOUSE SHINES OUTWARD

I have been in one small group or another continuously for
more than 30 years now. The idea of going out to serve in the
community has always seemed foreign at first, but I have discovered that groups that don't reach outside of themselves don't
last long. They typically turn inward and become consumed
with the stress of their own interpersonal problems. Relational
conflict will eventually erode a group from the inside out.

Each group is a potential lighthouse with the combined
brilliance of each member's spiritual flashlight pointed into
the spiritually darkened community. The powerful light of the
Spirit of God in us has the capacity to shine far beyond itself.
Groups that are not focusing outwardly can easily end up shining those flashlights into the eyes of one another. That can easily prove to be distracting if not dangerous.

The local church, whatever its size, doesn't seem to make
sense unless it is giving itself away to the world around it. I know
of a group that began reaching out to the homeless in a neighborhood park. They prepared meals for several dozen people
and offered coffee and conversation afterward. Their willingness to step out and serve was gradually rewarded with increased momentum. After two years, they were still reaching
out regularly to the homeless, with an annual budget of
$35,000 that they raised through tithing and donations.

The church begins to function as the church when we reach
out into the community. I can think of several reasons why we
ought to reach out.

Jesus Launched the Church Through a Small Group

The church of Jesus Christ looked fairly unimpressive in the
first chapter of Acts. After three years of training and modeling,
Jesus was taken up before His disciples to return to the Father.

They must have stood on the Mount of Olives staring up in both awe and shock: awe because they were in the presence of the glory of God, but also stunned and amazed at the final words of Jesus when He offered His strategy for winning the world: "You will be witnesses to me" (Acts 1:8).

At that moment this small group of disciples probably felt far from being empowered witnesses for Christ. They must have felt more like fearful failures. Things hadn't been going so well recently. One of their friends had betrayed Jesus and eventually committed suicide. The authorities were making threats and possibly coming after them. And now, wouldn't you know it, Jesus had departed for good! I think they were so shocked that they didn't know what to do next. Finally a couple of angels appeared and reiterated the words of Jesus: They were to return to Jerusalem and wait for the Lord's empowering.

This was just a small group, not so very different from some groups you and I have been a part of. For three years they watched Jesus bend the laws of nature with His miracles, speak the very words of God to the masses, and even raise the dead. For the past 40 days, they had witnessed the resurrected Jesus walk through walls and witness to the Spirit's power to bring the dead back to life through faith in God. Things seemed to be moving toward a crescendo.

At last, on the hillside outside Jerusalem, Jesus gives His secret for touching the world with the power of God: "You 11 will be my witnesses." They must have thought they heard wrong. I can just imagine the disciples saying something like, "He couldn't have said we would be His witnesses. Why, just look at us! We're shaking like leaves. We can't give His kingdom away. That would never work. Angels would be much better at this than us. They don't get scared and they're so much more mobile, being able to fly and all."

"He couldn't have said we would be His witnesses.
Why, just look at us! We're shaking like leaves.
We can't give His kingdom away. That would never
work. Angels would be much better at this than us.
They don't get scared and they're so much more
mobile, being able to fly and all."

They shouldn't have been all that surprised. Jesus had already made it apparent that He really likes to minister in small groups. The apostles had been part of a small group for the past three years. With the exception of a few miracles, all of Jesus' works had been done in the presence of His small group, the apostles. Jesus had encouraged them to travel about ministering in groups as well because the life of the Holy Spirit is energized when two or three are gathered in His name (see Matt. 18:20). If the world would be won, the life of God would go forward through small bands of people truly loving one another and sharing that love with others.

Shared Outreach Experiences Knit a Group Together

When groups focus beyond themselves, lives are changed and bettered, from the first person we pray for, feed or serve. "Remember when" stories provide a solid core of growth. A deep spiritual power permeates a group when they share a mission beyond themselves. The incarnational life of God flows through them to create an environment that builds a sense of family. When someone sees God move through him or her and that moment occurs in the presence of others, a special bonding takes place. That experience is frozen in time as a unique moment in spiritual history. Your group will never be the same after they have gone out into the community to minister together.

Outreach Raises the Level of Spiritual Health in Members' Lives
From the beginning, all of our groups had one or more special people we affectionately called EGRs—"Extra Grace Required." This helpful term coined by Dale Galloway describes individuals who have lots of special needs. Most of the time, this sort of person has more issues than a group can take on successfully. All EGRs will show some improvement when attention is shown them and they do tend to get better, gradually and slowly.

If unchecked and not given boundaries, an energetic EGR can actually kill a healthy group. I've seen it happen occasionally. As a hurting person enters a group and gives off distress signals, the group takes that person on as an assignment. If they are not careful, however, the purpose of the group can become getting that person healed. Most EGRs are probably never going to be fully healed in the context of the group. They've been peculiar for a long time and they may be that way the rest of their lives.

We need to signal to needy group members that we expect them to get better by giving themselves away along with the rest of us. Perhaps they aren't capable of doing sophisticated outreach that requires much emotional energy, but just about anyone can wash a windshield. I invited one older woman out with us who had been through some very traumatic episodes. I told her that she would probably see an increase in the grace of God in her life as she gave herself away to others in greater need than herself. Since she couldn't physically manage washing windshields, I put her in charge of passing out the squeegees and refilling the bottles of cleaning liquid. At the end of the day, she agreed that the life of God had touched her as she reached out with the good news.

An Action Orientation Helps to Identify Budding Leaders
What is a leader? A simple functional definition is "someone who leads others." In our day, the word brings to mind the

person with the most information or the one with the longest time spent as a Christian. In some groups it would be the one who graduated from a respected school. All these marks are good and even part of the picture, but in the end it's the one who leads who is truly a leader.

Nature versus nurture has long been debated in church circles. One group says, "We can produce a leader out of anyone provided they're given adequate oversight." The other group would disagree by saying, "Leaders are born, not made." My experience causes me to fall between these two opinions. I don't think just anyone can be shaped into a leader without some natural gifting. On the other hand, no one will lead effectively without help from mature and godly believers.

Arguments aside, that mysterious quality called leadership becomes clear when group momentum picks up steam. When activity commences, those who must lead come forth. If a fire were to erupt in a movie theater, the leader would be the one who knew the way out of the building. A leader is simply the person who knows the next step the group needs to take.

The person who is excited about what's going on, who comes early and stays late, who gives sacrificially, who is available—those are the identifiable marks of someone being raised up by the Lord as a leader in servant evangelism.

We can offer potential leaders a test to measure their personality type and background to see if they fit the general picture of a leader, or we can take a more practical approach. Groups that focus on giving themselves away will spontaneously produce leaders. It becomes obvious who is leading in a group that is doing ministry. The person who is excited about what's going on, who comes early and stays late, who gives sacrificially, who is available—those are the identifiable marks of someone being raised up by the Lord as a leader in servant evangelism.

Most People Are Too Shy to Do Outreach by Themselves

The concept of sharing the good news of Jesus Christ usually prompts thoughts of "personal evangelism." The common scenario involves one lone individual sharing Christ with an unbeliever. I often ask the participants of my seminars on evangelism what percentage of them regularly engage in some form of evangelism. Such an impromptu survey consistently reveals that less than 25 percent are regularly sharing Christ, and of those, a very small number have actually experienced praying with someone to ask Christ into their lives.

In short, the evangelical church in America is not very evangelical. We could hazard a pretty safe bet that effective and widespread outreach will not happen with individual Christians going out into the community. It is just too scary for most people to step out in this way. We've all heard that there is safety in numbers. I've discovered more importantly that there is courage to do evangelism in numbers.

For many years, I helped train small-group leaders of a multi ethnic church on the East Coast. The total membership of about 1,000 at the time was made up of some 25 different ethnic and language groups. Clustering them according to their native languages seemed to make the foreign city less foreboding.

The Filipino groups had a great desire to win their fellow compatriots to Christ, but found it difficult to make connections because of the hustle and bustle of the city. Conventional personal evangelism seemed too forward and unnatural for their cultural values. Because high blood pressure is a common genetic problem that runs in their families, these groups came

up with the idea of doing blood pressure checks in the entry-
ways of large apartment buildings frequented by other Fili-
pinos. Now, these groups are meeting dozens of their fellow cit-
izens with each outreach and are able to invite them into their
group's social events.

Doors of Opportunity Will Open for a Group

As we use groups to reach out into our communities, we can
affect neighbors we'd never be able to get in touch with on our
own. A small-group leader in our church had been trying to figure out a way to evangelize his upper-middle-class neighborhood on Cincinnati's north side for several years. He rejected
conventional methods as offensive to that population, most of
whom are overworked and tired. After living in the same house
for three years, this man still didn't know most of the neighbors
around him and they didn't seem interested in talking to him.

One evening, instead of their regular meeting format, everyone in his group was issued a dozen light bulbs and sent into
the neighborhood. As they went from house to house, the members identified themselves as part of the group that met at this
man's house and offered each homeowner a free light bulb just
to show God's love in a practical way. The people in the neighborhood opened up immediately! Lots of positive comments
were reported later on, but most importantly, this man became
known throughout his neighborhood as the "light-bulb guy."
People also knew that this guy was a Christian, that a group
met at his house, and that these people put their money where
their mouth was.

Our Impact Is Greater When We Work in Groups

Servant evangelism projects draw attention because of their nov-
elty, but a team also presents the appearance of being all over
the place. When our budding church had just a few dozen

members, four to eight of them would typically show up whenever we sponsored an outreach project. One Saturday morning, we had three people doing a free windshield wash at one location. A block away, we had another group of three going door to door raking leaves. As I washed their windshields, several people asked, "Are you with those people down the street who are raking leaves? How big is your church anyway? You people are *everywhere*." We were actually just a handful.

> *"Are you with those people down the*
> *street who are raking leaves? How big is*
> *your church anyway? You people*
> *are* everywhere. *"*

More recently, a group of about 20 participated in four different projects at a shopping area near downtown. We managed to intersect more than 1,000 people during our 90-minute outreach and truly gave the impression of being a massive army. When Christians decide to reach out, we become like the tiny mustard seed that grows and spreads into the community beyond all proportion. Even with small numbers, we can get the attention of the world around us.

The Life of Christ Shines Brightly Through a Group

Serving in a group creates an *atmosphere* of evangelism with joy as the primary byproduct. The Spirit of Christ, the ultimate servant, fills us and surrounds us in a way that is very appealing to outsiders. Paul describes that presence as the "fragrance of Christ among those who are being saved and among those who are perishing" (2 Cor. 2:15). Although they probably can't give words to its reality, our goal is to create a tangible experience of God's love as people encounter the life of Christ in us.

I heard about one young man who became convinced of the reality of God's life through encountering a small group. A Christian friend had patiently explained the good news of Christ to this fellow on several occasions, but he seemed unresponsive. On his way out the door to do some shopping, this nonbeliever finally exclaimed to his Christian buddy, "Look, I'm not going to listen to any more of what you have to say until you so-called Christians begin to show this love you're telling me about. I've heard about all the talk I can take."

Literally, at that very moment, they heard a knock at the door. They opened it to find part of a small group giving away light bulbs as a servant evangelism project. When he was greeted with, "Hi, I'd like to give you a light bulb to show you God's love in a practical way," the young man was stunned. Guess what was at the top of his shopping list? Light bulbs. He got what he insisted was necessary before he'd believe—*experiencing* the love of God through Christians. A few days later this man came to Christ and began attending the same church as the small group.

One small group of about 10 people would go out to a popular bicycle path every other Sunday afternoon to serve Gatorade to bikers and walkers. For the few minutes each passerby stood there and drank the Gatorade, they were in the presence of the Lord through His people. Even through a brief conversation, they could watch the believers in action and see how they related to the public and one another.

On one "Gatorade outing," some group members left the area for a few minutes. When they returned, they clearly noticed something around the outreach area. Even a few feet away felt entirely different, but up close to the Gatorade jug they felt a clear sense of the presence of the Lord. When several of our lights are shining at once, they take on added brilliance.

How Can Small Groups Begin Doing Kindness Evangelism?

Small groups function more effectively according to certain guidelines. Here are a few practical thoughts we learned from our own experience on how to launch groups into the community.

Discover What Projects Will Work for Your Group
It is important that a group feel ownership of this approach in general and any particular projects you decide to undertake. Discuss the philosophy behind servant evangelism and brainstorm as to what might work in your neck of the woods. Because people's needs tend to be quite different from place to place, what flies in one part of town might go over like a lead balloon just a few blocks away. Ask God for wisdom.

Your small group may already have its finger on the pulse of the community more clearly than your church leaders, who tend to focus more on meeting the needs of the members. Ask yourselves as a group what needs are present in your circles of influence. Begin to address those that are immediately clear. Once you've seized those opportunities, more clarity will come to you. Before long you'll be tapped into the unique projects that fit your community.

Don't Pressure the Local Church Leadership to Take Charge
Most pastors welcome evangelistic efforts but simply don't have the time or emotional stamina to lead something else personally. Depending on the local church government, obtain the minimal amount of permission required by explaining to the pertinent leaders what you have in mind. Then step out and begin to serve. Your success is the fastest way to spread this outreach among other groups. As good stories begin to circulate, you'll get the attention and affirmation of the church leaders.

Go Out Once Every Four to Six Weeks

Each group needs to decide how often they can go out to do ministry projects without overextending themselves. Our groups don't necessarily meet every week; some meet twice or even once per month depending on the schedules and needs of the members. I recommend that you go out once every fourth or fifth time you meet. If you meet just twice a month, that means you'd go out about every other month for a project. If your group meets every week, you'd go out about once a month. Because of the hurried pace of life most of us face, you'll probably find it necessary to exchange one of your normal meeting times for an outreach project. We all have lots of "good things" happening in our lives. It's difficult to get excited about another event being added on top of an already stressed-out schedule.

If You Are a Leader, Give Your Group Permission to Minister

Leaders of small groups need to *regularly* give people permission to go out into the community to do ministry. They also need to keep explaining that such involvement is perfectly fine for laypeople. Most Christians have to unlearn the centuries-old mentality of waiting for the clergy or trained professionals to lead the way. Martin Luther wanted to see each believer view himself or herself as a priest or minister, but sadly that aspect of the Reformation has never taken hold. Few pastors would object to having their people doing ministry in the community.

Value Spontaneity

It isn't all that complicated to show deeds of kindness. Sometimes I find it refreshing to surprise everyone in the group by dropping the normal weekly plan and going out to serve. (Not all groups I've been in like being surprised, so use wisdom here.) Some of our most positive experiences have risen out of observing a need and then reasoning, "Hey, we could do something about that need. Let's go help!"

A woman in one of our groups noticed that many women shoppers at a local, self-serve grocery were trying to simultaneously pack their grocery bags, tend to their children and write a check. Most of them happily saved money on groceries at this store, but getting out the door was difficult. The group leader went to the store manager and offered to have some of his people pack bags at the checkout stand, while others escorted the shoppers to their cars and helped unload the groceries. These simple services were greatly appreciated.

Don't Tire People with Long Projects
One important practical note: When you go out as a group, it's wise to usually keep your outings to a maximum of two hours. The idea here is to go out long enough to do some significant serving, but to finish your projects before it becomes work. For many of us, that crossover point occurs at two hours. Much beyond two hours also becomes more difficult for most people to schedule into their lives on any regular basis.

I recommend that you begin any two-hour project with a brief time of instruction and conclude with a possible time of debriefing at the end, bringing your total time to about two and a half hours. We usually gathered at 9:45 on Saturday mornings, were gone by 10 o'clock, and then gathered back at a given location at noon to share stories of how things went.

Consider Funding Your Own Projects Within the Group
If your church doesn't have enough money to fund your projects, take up a little offering among yourselves for equipment and supplies. Most of the ideas contained in appendix 1 are simple and low in cost. If you need equipment, I recommend that you not put an expectation upon the church as a whole to

finance your outreach. This idea is rather unusual. It may easily take some time to convince the leaders that servant evangelism succeeds at touching people with God's love. A small investment in simple equipment will enable you to launch out. When the fruit becomes more apparent, perhaps local church financing will become available.

Don't Worry About Mistakes

Remember that God blesses action and obedience, even if you make mistakes! He loves to provide guidance, but we must take the first step. If you are a group leader, don't spend much time worrying about success or failure. Just getting out on the streets counts as a major success no matter how your outreach project goes. The anointing of the Lord will rest upon those who are willing to take the risk of bringing the love of God to others.

Mistakes are predictable in any new endeavor, but a group outreach helps us to feel less vulnerable. Most of my greatest learning experiences in evangelism have come as I stepped out, and failed, in the safety of a group.

My first face-to-face contact with the needy came on Christmas Eve with a small group of five men. I had never actually gone into a poor area to see firsthand how some people live. I had no idea how to proceed. I had never read anything on the subject, but I was willing to step out because I was convinced that God loves the poor. As we draw near to those He particularly wants to reach, we will experience the Holy Spirit empowering us to minister more effectively.

On this particular morning, we first gathered for prayer and instruction. One man in the group asked, "Steve, how do you minister to the poor anyway?"

I said, "Just watch me. This is simple."

Sometimes it's best to just step out in boldness. When I knocked on the first door, I heard three deadbolts turn. The woman behind the door peered out through two chains. "Yeah, what do you want?" By this time all four team members were looking over my shoulder, paying close attention to my every word and move. After all, I was the one who said I knew how to minister to the needy.

"We were just wondering, *are you poor?*"

I don't know what got into me. I realize now how incredibly insensitive my words were and I'm still amazed that this woman didn't call the police on us. But in spite of my lack, this woman was touched and unchained the door.

With tears in her eyes, she told us her story. Just the night before, she and her five children were praying for God to send them some sort of Christmas. On Christmas Eve, they still had no money for a celebration. The father had taken off with the rent money and was, she suspected, drinking somewhere.

As we left that home, it was difficult to figure out who had been more profoundly touched: the "ministers" in the small group or the family who so joyfully received our food and gifts.

We brought with us an entire Christmas setup—presents for several kids, food, and even a Christmas tree complete with ornaments. As we left that home, it was difficult to figure out who had been more profoundly touched: the "ministers" in the small group or the family who so joyfully received our food and gifts.

MORE KINDNESS

Something happens when people go out with others to serve their community. An established home group or a group created just for the purpose of serving can set aside a day a week to mow lawns or pass out bottles of water. Sharing an assignment helps us focus beyond ourselves.

In the years I have been in groups, I have discovered that focusing outward deepens a group's inward commitment to each other. Also, I have discovered that some of the best ideas pop onto the radar screen when as a group we have been out serving others. Our creative juices seem to function at their highest capacity when we are focused outward rather than inward.

Come together to love your neighbors and see what God does in your midst. His power will stir up in you and flow through you.

CHAPTER 10

Displaying the Pearl

*One person with a belief is equal to a force of ninety-nine
who only have an interest.*
JOHN STUART MILL

*There was a man, though some did count him mad,
the more he cast away the more he had.*
JOHN BUNYAN

Several years ago in Brazil, some children who were playing in a
junkyard found a silver metal container. Someone cracked it
open to reveal the most exquisite blue, round blob nesting inside. It was different from anything they'd ever seen. It glowed
even in the daylight!

Before long, a crowd had gathered to look at the glowing
ball. Everybody wanted to hold this odd substance. One man
dipped his finger in it and wrote his initials on his bare chest.
Another couple of people played catch with it like it was a
rubber ball. Another man worked the pliable ball into various
shapes while the crowd around him laughed.

Later that day, strange symptoms began to appear on the
bodies of all the people who had touched the blue ball. Each
person began to feel chilled, feverish and generally weak. Every
bit of skin that had come into contact with this glowing glob
had burn marks. Within 24 hours the man who had written his
initials on his chest had deep burns etched into his skin.

After some investigation, it was discovered that the canister had been illegally discarded by a medical equipment company. The contents had at one time been used to save lives by treating cancer. The highly radioactive material was never intended to be touched by human hands. Within a week all of the people who had handled the contents of the canister were dead, victims of radioactive poisoning.

Radioactivity is extremely powerful. In the right environment this power brings life; improperly applied, it can bring great harm and even death. Jesus approached the power of the kingdom of God in similar terms in this parable: "The kingdom of heaven is like a merchant seeking beautiful pearls, who, when he had found one pearl of great price, went and sold all that he had and bought it" (Matt. 13:45-46).

Jesus used the rarest pearl to represent the enormous treasure a believer finds in relationship with God. When we experience the goodness of God, we become willing to pay whatever price is necessary to enter into His family. And in repenting and coming to Jesus, we do lose all to find the pearl. As Paul says, we "count all things loss for the excellence of the knowledge of Christ" (Phil. 3:8).

It would be unnatural to find the most unusual pearl in the world only to hide it from view. Such a rare treasure is something to get excited about! Who in their right mind would want to keep such a fabulous find to themselves? Those who own much jewelry know that pearls especially need to be worn regularly to keep their luster. If not exposed to fresh air they eventually grow discolored and begin to disintegrate.

Most of you have experienced the awesome beauty of the pearl of which Jesus spoke. Do you know that this pearl, if held onto and not shared, can produce a toxic counterfeit of Christianity? Jesus referred to the Pharisees as "hypocrites," "whitewashed tombs which indeed appear beautiful outwardly, but inside are full of dead men's bones and all uncleanness" (Matt. 23:27). These men had hidden the pearl in a cloak of religious rules and regulations so airtight that only the nearly perfect dared come into the temple.

What we do with the pearl of great price reveals our deepest attitudes. If we hold onto it with a stingy heart, the kingdom of heaven can disintegrate around us. If that which was intended to be displayed outwardly is clutched to ourselves, our hearts can suffer spiritual decay and even death.

God's heart has always been inclusive.
He has always provided a place for outsiders
to hear about His mercy.

Jesus ran into another group of people who were hoarding the pearl (see John 2:13-16). If you look in the maps section of your Bible, you may find a layout of the temple in Jerusalem. The outermost portion was designated as the "Court of the Gentiles" where non-Jews could hear teaching on the one true God. We can see in this arrangement that God's heart has always been inclusive. He has always provided a place for outsiders to hear about His mercy.

In Jesus' day, this area of the temple had been taken over by the religious rulers and designated as a place for exchanging money and selling animals to be used in the temple sacrifices. Because of their action, the pearl of great price had been locked away in the temple so that outsiders were excluded from experiencing the grandeur of God's love.

Jesus became furious with these temple leaders. His anger drove Him to the point that He expelled the moneychangers from the temple, turned over their tables, and scattered their animals. It seems ironic that the Messiah, the Prince of Peace, expressed such tremendous anger in this particular setting. I believe that Jesus was displaying the heart of God in a way that we've seldom seen. Nothing makes God angrier than people who keep the pearl from being displayed for the world to see.

The cleansing of the temple launched Jesus' public ministry. For the next three years, He served with an attitude opposite to that of the excluding temple leaders. Jesus put wheels on the pearl. Wherever He went, His goal was to display the glory and majesty of God. The Son of God knew that when outsiders saw the beauty of this divine relationship clearly displayed, they would be attracted to the family of God.

Our call is the same: to take the pearl of great price, attach wheels to it, and take it out into the community. The incarnation manifests this same reality: God coming among humankind. Our tendency to hide this pearl has plagued the Church in every generation of believers. Let's see what we can learn by considering a group with passion for God but little practical expression of that life to the world.

The Church of Laodicea: Be Hot or Cold!

Chapters 2 and 3 of the Revelation of John contain letters to the seven primary churches in what was then called Asia Minor (modern Turkey). These groups were for the most part rebuked for failures in their attitudes. One of them was located in the city of Laodicea, famous around the world for its eye salve. This ointment was highly sought after because it brought welcome relief from eye infections so common in that day.[1] Jesus is referring to this salve when He recommends they take some of their own medicine so that they will be able to see clearly (see Rev. 3:18).

Two key elements were necessary to produce this salve: very hot and very cold water. In the hills surrounding Laodicea, a natural spring bubbled with both hot and cold water. Their salve put this city on the map, but there was one problem: Production was severely limited by their outmoded means of manufacturing. The factory in Laodicea could not keep up with the demand for the famous salve.

The city leaders proposed a plan to upscale their factory and capitalize on the demand for their product. Taxes were increased, private money was invested, and before long, a huge new factory had been built in the center of Laodicea. An elaborate conduit system, considered advanced for that day, transported the hot and cold water right into the factory. At last the grand opening took place, and at the big moment the conduits were flooded with water from the hillside springs.

Because of the enormous financial investment, what happened next must have been incredibly anticlimactic. To everyone's shock, the very hot water had cooled down to just lukewarm by the time it flowed into the new factory. The very cold water had warmed up in the conduit to also become just lukewarm. The production process for this eye salve was unforgiving: both very hot and very cold water were absolutely necessary. Now, after such an investment of time and money, all they had was lukewarm water.

In my reading of these seven letters in Revelation, the most striking message is given to the church of Laodicea. If the first six received correction, this last church received a double-barreled rebuke: "I know your works, that you are neither cold nor hot. I wish you were cold or hot. So then, because you are lukewarm, and neither cold nor hot, I will spew you out of my mouth" (Rev. 3:15-16).

These words have been often quoted by evangelists as meaning, "get hot for God or else!" Or get cold with Him, which is to be against Him, because it's better to be clearly against God and His kingdom than to play games. Lukewarm is taken to mean hypocrisy—the person who says they belong to Christ but whose life betrays the fact that they really don't. The typical modern interpretation is that we ought to be living a "hot" brand of Christianity or we will ultimately be vomited from the mouth of God.

> *Lukewarmness doesn't mean a lack of excitement or commitment to God; rather it is a void of usefulness. To be lukewarm is to fail at making our Christianity real.*

When John's letter was read by the Laodicean believers, they understood a very different message. "Because you are lukewarm, and neither cold nor hot, I will spew you out of my mouth." The church in Laodicea understood instantly the call of the resurrected Christ. In saying, "I could wish you were cold or hot," Jesus was saying in essence, *"Be useful* in My kingdom." Both hot and cold were equally useful in the making of eye salve. Lukewarm was totally useless.

Lukewarmness doesn't mean a lack of excitement or commitment to God; rather it is a void of usefulness. To be lukewarm is to fail at making our Christianity real. So what does a useful Christian life look like? A few believers are called to live out their faith as contemplatives who spend the bulk of their time in prayer—an extremely useful vocation in the kingdom of God. Most of us are called to a more action-oriented approach to following Christ.

A pastor friend of mine relayed a story that happened when he was leading a service project. This group was washing windshields in the parking lot of a grocery store. One clean-cut young guy walked up to a four-by-four truck with a couple of really rough guys staring at him. With gusto he asked the driver, "How would you like it if I washed your windshield free to show you God's love?"

The man responded back, "How would you like it if I broke your arm to show you God's love? Stay away from my truck!"

The young Christian remained undaunted and answered back, "You don't understand. We're doing this to show you God's love in a way that will meet a need in your life. We're not taking money; we're here because Jesus loves you."

This truck driver didn't quite know how to respond. He just stared for a moment with his mouth agape. He then slowly replied, "Oh, I get it. Two thousand years ago Jesus washed people's feet. Now you're kind of doing the same thing by washing my windshield. Sure, you can wash my windshield."

GONZO CHRISTIANITY

Enormous opportunity stands before us right now, even at our very doorstep. As we uncover the hunger for spiritual reality in America, we can choose to either watch or jump in as "gonzo Christians." Hunter Thompson, a colorful American journalist and author, coined "gonzo journalism" to describe his unusual approach to covering a news story. Instead of writing from the outside as a neutral observer, Thompson's goal was to cover an event from the inside as a participant. He took his paper and pencil and jumped into the middle of the crowd.

Today is the day for an army of gonzo Christians to come to the forefront of the Church. The days of watching, listening, studying the end times, and arguing our point about when Jesus is *really* coming back are over! This heartfelt desire to win the world for Christ was driven home one morning with a friend of mine while he was jogging. He was running alone, using the time for devotional prayer, telling the Lord how

much he loved Him, when he sensed the Lord speak to him.
The Holy Spirit seemed to say, "You spend all your time trying
to figure out how to get off the earth when I'm trying to get you
on the earth!"

What sorts of attitudes will allow us to be useful in displaying the pearl? As gonzo Christians, we need to be peculiar people willing to take on these same attitudes.

"Greater Is He . . ."
We must make a commitment to take the pearl out to those
who live beyond the church walls. We will never succeed unless
we believe that "he who is in you is greater than he who is in the
world" (1 John 4:4). I don't know any Christian who doesn't
officially believe that verse, but most believers I know have
never put this truth to the test. We will never discover the greatness of Him who is in us until we go into the world with the
good news. We will never know the greatness of the light unless
we shine our light into the surrounding darkness.

---

*We will never discover the greatness of Him who is
in us until we go into the world with the good news.*

For years, I kept my goals so small and easily attainable that
they didn't require the blessing of God upon them to materialize. Now my desire is to live out a Christian life that requires
that "greater than" promise of power. In Cincinnati, I believe
that we will see a day in the near future when various fellowships
around the city will have mobilized enough to touch one-tenth
of the city each year. Over a several year period, most of this city
will be reached with acts of love and charity. What is going on
in Cincinnati could be done in every city in the country.

A friend of mine pastors an evangelical church in Fort Collins, Colorado. His church has mobilized about 100 people who go into the community about once a month doing deeds of kindness. That group of 100 could easily touch half of their city each year with the love of God. It won't take long for them to literally saturate their city with deeds of love. Pretty soon they'll be known all over town as "the people who serve others."

Reckless Abandon to the Cause of Christ

Several years ago, I saw a movie called *Red Dawn*, a thought-provoking film, though probably a bit reactionary. The story follows the exploits of a band of high schoolers who are trying to survive a foreign invasion of their Colorado town. Overnight they must make the transformation from being self-centered teenagers into being soldiers who survive against the toughest odds.

Although reckless at first, bit by bit they grow smarter and stronger until they eventually take on entire enemy battalions with ease. The key for these high-schoolers is their willingness to take risks. They realize that most of the important lessons of warfare are learned in the wake of disaster.

In just the same way, we must be willing to grow in our ministry skill as we go along. The key in servant evangelism is to just get started. If we demand a risk-free brand of Christianity, we certainly won't grow and we won't be effective in reaching the world around us. Those who claim to be ministry experts and haven't yet experienced significant failure scare me. I don't trust them because I know that risk and pain accompany any significant progress in reaching out with the good news of Jesus Christ.

Luke explains that his gospel account told the story of "all that Jesus *began* both to do and teach" (Acts 1:1). Jesus launched His ministry, which was then carried on by the church that He instituted. Their call was to do the works of Jesus—to feed, clothe, visit, give cold water, speak the truth, give encouragement.

Jesus tells a parable in Matthew 25 about two groups of people—which He calls sheep and goats—who were being tested. Neither of them knew they were encountering Jesus when they saw the needy. He praises the sheep who did the works of compassion and kindness; He reprimands and punishes the goats who did not do those works.

The key in servant evangelism is to just get started. If we demand a risk-free brand of Christianity, we certainly won't grow and we won't be effective in reaching the world around us.

We identify ourselves as either sheep or goats by the way we respond to the hurting around us. Many years ago, I met a group of about 10 Christians who had gathered together out of a desire to reach the community in practical ways with the mercy, grace and love of God. It was exciting for me to be with them because they were open to doing whatever it would take to accomplish their goal.

My encouragement to them was to first get a feel for the needs of the people of their city. They needed to ask themselves, "Where in our city would a helping hand, a free bag of groceries, a timely coin in a parking meter, or a cold drink make a difference?" Squeaky wheels can be found all around us if we would just listen.

This small group took my counsel and eagerly began to develop a strategy for reaching out to the unchurched. They weren't satisfied with just inviting people to meetings. Before long they had provided food for single moms, sponsored a major clothing drive for needy school children, given away free school supplies, put on language clinics for immigrants, and offered financial counseling to those in economic difficulties. They began to bring the Kingdom out into the community.

When I spoke with this group some time later, I was amazed to see what the Lord had been doing in their midst. These people had really been doing the works of the sheep! They had grown in just four years to the largest church in town with more than 700 members. People were coming to Christ regularly. They had started another church in a nearby city, with plans to start two more during the next two years. Equally exciting to me were the number of people in the community who were being touched with kindness and the number of Christians who wanted to continue reaching out with the mercy, grace and love of God.

PAVING A ROAD OF LOVE
AND ACCEPTANCE

One Labor Day, we held a free car wash. We had tried car washes at different locations—gas stations, malls, grocery stores and even bank parking lots on holidays. Our favorite spot was a place on the north side of Cincinnati called Jenny's Sportsbar. Best known for their country music and "meanest man" contests, this bar advertises on several popular FM radio stations.

We had washed several dozen cars on this particular day when a man cruised in at the wheel of a flashy new import. He hopped out of the car and we went to work. As the "designated evangelist" at the moment, I began to explain why we were washing his car for free. This man smiled, nodded in approval, and then said, "So who do I make out my check to?"

"You don't understand, sir. We aren't taking money for this car wash. We just want to show you God's love in a practical way," I said. I repeated this explanation three times before he finally got it. I could tell because his expression changed: He lit up, his eyes got big, and his mouth was hanging open. By my fourth explanation, he was all ears.

Then he did something that I have seen several times when doing servant evangelism. This man began to confess his failures to me right there in the parking lot of Jenny's Sportsbar. He told me about his sexual escapades, his lack of church attendance, and yet his awareness of God's presence over the years. He told me that he had been a starting pitcher for a National League baseball team until suffering a career-ending knee injury.

This was an amazing turn of events. In just a couple of minutes, I had encountered this man at a very deep level. He had just shared several intimate secrets of his heart with a total stranger. Our kindness had paved a road of love and acceptance for this man. His response spoke of a sincere desire to reconnect with this God who had taken time to seek him out.

There is only one more thing you need to do to join God's conspiracy of kindness. Put this book down, pick up a squeegee, and start washing windshields.

There is only one more thing you need to do to join God's conspiracy of kindness. Put this book down, pick up a squeegee, and start washing windshields. I would enjoy sharing more with you about bringing God's love to your community, but I've run out of time. In five minutes I'm meeting some friends to go and wash windshields at a grocery store parking lot. If you were here, I'd offer you a squeegee and have you come along. We'd have great fun!

MORE KINDNESS

Jesus is shown more profoundly to the culture around us through acts of love than by any other means.

The pearl Jesus spoke of is one that is seen, touched or smelled—not something that is merely read about in a story. It is *embodied*. Once people catch the hunger for the pearl, they will do anything possible—*everything* possible—to own the pearl. Onlookers think owners of the pearl are a bit crazy . . . make that completely crazy.

A good friend of mine, Martin, is a veteran church planter from Switzerland. Over the past 15 years, he has built the largest church in that country by going into his city and loving the postmodern skeptics around him. Amazingly, he has found favor with the majority of his city. In a country where spiritual decline has been taking place for many generations, Martin and his church have served their way into the hearts of hundreds of thousands again and again.

Recently he and his wife moved to Berlin to do it all over again. That city is also spiritually dark and very skeptical. Martin's approach to capturing the attention of the people? Their team of a couple dozen don bright construction vests that read "Doggie Dirt Clean Up Crew" across the back (in German of course!). Berlin, a city of several million, is known for its high population of dog owners who love their pets and take them on walks. In contrast to many U.S. cities that have strict laws regarding such things, doggie dirt is common on the sidewalks. The crews stop by shop owners, introduce themselves, give them a connect card and get to work.

Though they have only been at it for a couple of months, they have been in the news several times. After all, this is a man-bites-dog story (pardon the pun—couldn't resist!). I'm not a prophet, but my guess is it won't be long before there are several thousand Doggie Dirt scoopers all over Berlin who are defining the real Jesus, the in-the-flesh Jesus, to this skeptical city. Don't be surprised if you see a story on your evening news about Martin, being himself and living like Jesus at the same time.

Note

1. Laverne Tengborn, "An Historical, Cultural, Geographical, Exegetical Study of Revelation 2 and 3," Doctoral Dissertation for Lutheran Bible Institute, Los Angeles, CA, 1977.

CHAPTER 11

The Power of Now

I receive about 200 personal emails each day, and one of the common questions I get is, "Am I called to reach out?" When I read this, I realize that I am connecting with a person who is more emotional than objective. As far as the Scriptures are concerned, the matter is crystal clear. It's not a matter of some people having the gift of evangelism while others don't.

I have made this statement to hundreds of thousands of pastors, seminary students, seminary professors and denominational leaders over the years. Not surprisingly, many have disagreed with me and have even claimed that the Scriptures teach that evangelism is a spiritual gift. When I was younger I used to spend time and energy arguing with sisters and brothers like this. I am officially done arguing. I now just smile and give them my email address and explain, "There is an office of Evangelist as Ephesians 4 explains, but there is no mention anywhere in Scripture of a spiritual gift of evangelism. If I am wrong, I am thrilled to discover that you at long last—after hundreds of thousands of conversations over several decades—can point out a phantom verse I have somehow overlooked." I have received many follow-up emails, and 100 percent of them have been from leaders who had never noticed there is no such gift. As a result, their entire view of evangelism has done a 180-degree turnaround.

If all of us have been called to "do the work of an evangelist" as Paul wrote to Timothy, the task of evangelism is significantly different than what we have made it over the past few generations in the Western Church.

One of my primary mentors had a great motto. He said that he longed to see the Church become a place where "everyone gets to play!" In other words, that the Church would become a permission-giving place. In my 30-plus years in the U.S. Church, I have noticed that more often than not, it is necessary to jump through a lot of hoops (make that committees) in order to get the green light before we dare risk stepping out to do much of anything. Does that observation resonate with you? If so, why is that? The problem with being so risk-averse is that the kingdom of Jesus only goes forward as we are willing to take risks. The following are some ways to take smart risks that will bear fruit.

USE THE RIGHT TOOLS

In this book, I use golf clubs as a metaphor for the tools we must become familiar with if we seek evangelism fruitfulness. Like PGA professionals, we are in the "game" of reaching out continually. As you add new clubs to your golf bag, ask yourself, "Is this going to help me or encumber me along the way?"

I am working on a book now that reflects on my early attempts at outward-effectiveness. Early on, I confused arguing people into the Kingdom with answering people's questions. I read dozens of books that answered the questions that people were guaranteed to ask. Books along these lines continue to be written. Some of these are helpful, but some are actually counterproductive because they are:

1. *Discouraging.* Those who read such books get the idea that in order to be effective in evangelism one must

be a certain kind of person—a verbal intellectual. If
that is truly the case, the percentage of those who
can "play" includes fewer and fewer people.

2. *Misleading.* Many of the questions asked and answered are questions that already-believers tend to
ask. Sales records show that though some of these
books have sold well, the vast majority of sales have
been strictly to already-believers, not to not-yet
believers. You may think, *That's because believers are
giving them away.* That isn't exactly correct. Do some
research, and you'll discover that we are evangelizing the "already-convinced" with these books.

3. *Theoretical.* I am always interested in research and
development, in experimenting with new ideas and
approaches. However, I am not interested in theories that have not been put to a practical test.

Before you add another club to your bag, make sure that it
will help you play the game—that it is encouraging (everybody
gets to play!), accurate and practical.

LIVE OUT THE LAW OF LARGE NUMBERS

Over the years I have encouraged people to touch lots of people
in their various cities. I thought I was communicating clearly,
but apparently my idea of "lots" and theirs are vastly different.

A church with 100 people on an average weekend can realistically reach out to *100,000 people* in a year's time. Read that
last sentence again. If necessary, underline it or highlight it in
yellow until it sinks in. This is what I mean when I say, "Live out
the Law of Large Numbers." I mean *really* large.

Start small and go large. See appendix 1 for more ideas than you can use in one year. I promise, 100,000 is doable.

Leave the Monastery

I admittedly watched far too much TV in my youth. Near the top of my all-time favorite shows list was the series *Kung Fu*, starring David Carradine. Each week we watched as Carradine's character, Kwai Chang Caine, grew up under the mentoring of a blind kung fu master.

The famous test was simple: "Kwai Chang, when you can snatch pebble from hand, it is time for you to leave." The older blind man had lightning reflexes and won every week—until the student reached adulthood. The magic words then came: "Now it is time to go!"

We have operated under the illusion that the Church is like the monastery and our leaders are like the blind kung fu master.

> **There are no hidden secrets that
> take years to discover.**

If you are operating under that perception, you might want to check out the Mormon operation in Salt Lake City. They are very into secrets.

The second heresy to enter the Church was that of the Gnostics, who claimed to have special information regarding how to get into a special relationship with God. If one paid a special price or dedicated oneself to the special teachings of special teachers who had special insight that was gotten by special, secret means, you too could know the secret and special knowledge. As the Church Lady would say, "Isn't that special!"

Certainly, as each of us goes forward in a life following Jesus, we learn how to become more effective—but this is not

secret knowledge! At no point is there a red pill or blue pill. No
Kool-Aid. No special shoes. Just each of us loving Jesus more
and more and our neighbor as ourselves.

There is no correlation between lengthy preparation time and evangelism effectiveness.

Admittedly, I don't have scientific evidence in hand to prove my
point, but I do have plenty of anecdotal proof. I feel sure there
is a connection between the amount of training one has received
and evangelism effectiveness. My findings are not what you
might expect. I have found that *the more official training received,
the less effective one becomes in reaching out to not-yet believers.*

There is a high correlation between effectiveness in evangelism and putting into practice the obvious invitations in front of us.

My life in Jesus is now something over 30 years and counting,
and those decades, interestingly, are in three phases. I "drew my
first breath," if you will, with the clear understanding that I was
to live to see many come into Jesus' kingdom.

Decade One was spent arguing with lots of people. Not surprisingly, there was very little fruit. I ran off the majority of my
friends and hurt many of my family.

In Decade Two, I discovered the power of serving in the style
of Jesus. That is, I began to move through life moved by compassion. The problem early on was that I confined that serving to
mostly group settings. That is still a valid idea. It is a great way
to initiate people into a lifestyle of outwardness. As I see it, large-
scale serving projects are much like training wheels on a bicycle
that allow a child to get up and onto a bike. With training wheels,
the risk is lowered to the point that crashes are minimized.

In Decade Three, I have discovered that the great fruit is living in the "The Power of Now" as I call it. Instead of viewing kindness as a mindset that we take on and off, we simply go there and live there all the time. There is no "Off" switch. We live in the power of kindness all the time. Again, it is the power of God living through us, His kindness being manifest in and through us. We don't *try* to be kind. The sooner we give up all attempts at trying to be kind, the better. Why is this so?

Because no one is going to be touched in any sort of memorable way by human niceness.

Give up your attempts to do anything to help God. Simply confess to God that you are willing and available. Then listen, observe and expect invitations to join into others' lives. Opportunities will come—probably beginning today, unless you are reading this at home in the evening, and then we'll settle for a launch tomorrow! Let me pray with you right now:

Father, launch me into a life of living in
an atmosphere of kindness,
being ready, willing and able to the promptings
of the Holy Spirit
as I live out my life, day in and day out.
Let it be!

Epilogue

When *Conspiracy of Kindness* was first published, I had no idea that it would have the staying power it has turned out to have. Apparently kindness is doable! I have been thrilled to write many books—all on the topic of kindness! (You can check these out at www.servantevangelism.com and www.kindness.com.)

The concept of kindness opening the door to the heart seems to be a universal human truth. I have traveled through much of the world since *Conspiracy of Kindness* was published (by the way, it has come out in a number of languages). All indications are that people are universally vulnerable to the power of the kindness of God: "The kindness of God leads to repentance" (Rom. 2:4).

I have learned a handful of lessons since *Conspiracy of Kindness* first came out.

1. *Faithfulness counts.* Keep on keeping on in your acts of generosity no matter what the outcome seems at first. Usually the first attempt to serve one's way into the community is a slow start. In fact, in my experience, it takes about two years for the first people who are served to steadily make their way into church. But no matter! Your church will grow in the meantime just the same because you will be manifesting a winsomeness to your city that is very attractive.

2. *Small things done with great love will change the world.* I have given up on trying to do big things for God. I've come to this conclusion: All that counts is our attempts at small things done with faithfulness to

God over the long haul. When we attempt to do big things for God, more often than not we end up bringing glory to ourselves, and that not only doesn't count for God, but it also looks ridiculous.

3. *There are unlimited creative ways to share the love of Christ.* In Cincinnati, just when we thought, *Now that's the best idea we've had yet!* someone came along with another idea that was even more creative. People from all over the world are coming up with new ways to bring the love of Christ to their culture. I encourage you—get with your fellow servant evangelism friends over a cup of coffee on a regular basis and let your imaginations run wild by the power of the Holy Spirit.

4. *Just a few people can make a big difference.* It seems that all significant movements start with a small minority. Almost everywhere I go, I see servant evangelism start with a small group of people who are willing to roll up their sleeves and get some dirt under their finger-nails. Kindness is contagious. Small groups grow into large groups in time. Don't worry about your begin-nings. What started out as a few people in Cincinnati grew to more over the next few months. By the time we had planned our one-day event for several months, we had enlisted some 300 churches. In just a couple of hours, we reached out to over 300,000 people.

Focus on your goal: to touch and change your city with the love of Christ!

Steve Sjogren
Cincinnati, Ohio
Winter 2003

Servant Evangelism Projects That Work

If there is any kindness I can show, or any good thing I can do to any fellow being, let me do it now, and not deter or neglect it, as I shall not pass this way again.

WILLIAM PENN

All projects are free—no donations accepted! Some services are provided while those being served are away, making cards or printed notes necessary.

Public Places
(gas stations, restaurants, malls, grocery stores, retail stores, soccer and baseball fields, etc.)
Umbrella Escorts
Windshield Washing
Coffee Giveaways
Gift Wrapping at Christmas
Soft Drink Giveaways
Restroom Cleaning
Grocery Bag Loading Assistance
Bag Packing at Self-Serve Groceries
Grocery Cart Return

Sporting Events
Giveaways:
  Cokes
  Coffee
  Popcorn
  Popsicles
  Peanuts
  Sunglasses (cheap ones)
Windshield Washing

Automobiles
Check Oil and Fill
Single Mom's Oil Change
Washer Fluid Fill
Tire Pressure Check
Windshield Washing at Self-Serve Stations
Oil and Filter Change
Interior Vacuuming
Bulb Replacement
Car Wash
Free Fragrance Cards
Windshield Scrape or Sweep in Cold Weather (Apartment Complex)

Roadside/Drive-by
Summer Car Washes
Coke Giveaways
Winter Car Washes/Desalting
Popsicle Giveaways

Downtown/Business Districts
Windshield Washing
Umbrella Escort
Business Window Washing
Toilet Scrubbing
Soft Drink Giveaways
Free Cookies
Free Cappuccino
Feeding Parking Meters
Free Polaroid Photos at Carriage
  Rides
Free Shoe Shine

Parks
Doggie Dirt Clean-up
Helium Balloons for Kids
Polaroid Picture Giveaways
Popsicle Giveaways
Grilling Hot Dogs/Free Picnic
Gatorade at Biking Trails
Gatorade at Jogging Trails
Pictionary in the Park
Flower Seed Packets
Face Painting

College Campuses
Pen/Pencil Giveaways
Free Copies
Free Coffee, Soft Drinks
Dorm Cleaning
Free Tutoring
Gatorade or Lemonade in Hot
  Weather
Hot Chocolate in Cold Weather
Drink Giveaways at Intramural
  Events and Greek Sports Events
Breakfast Bagels or Pop Tarts

House to House
Leaf Raking
Lawn Mowing
Grass Edging
Screen Cleaning
General Yard Cleanup
Door-to-Door Carnation
  Giveaways
Potted Plant Giveaways
Flower Seed Packet Giveaways
Gutter Cleaning
Sidewalk Sweeping
Windshield Washing (Car in
  Driveway)
Sunday Morning Paper and
  Coffee Giveaways
Snow Removal from Walks and
  Drives
Empty Garbage Can Return
Kitchen Cleanup
Window Washing
Minor House Repairs
General Cleaning (Interior)
House Number Painting on Curbs
Free Community Dinner
Doggie Yard Cleanup
Light Bulb Replacement
Minor Tree Trimming
Weed Spraying/Pulling
Seal Blacktop Driveways
Scrape Fireplaces
Radon Detectors
Carbon Monoxide Detectors
Smoke Detector Batteries
Fragrance Spraying
Filter Change AC/Heat
Garage Cleaning
Free Fireplace Kindling
Bark and Mulch for Yards

Miscellaneous
Mother's Day Carnation
  Giveaways

Food Delivery to Shut-ins

Car Drying at Self-Serve Car Washes

Grocery Store Bag Packing

Free Bird Feeders and Refills to Convalescent Hospital Patients

Collect Trees after Christmas for Disposal

Free Bait at Local Fishing Spots

Free Coffee at a Major Bus or Subway Stop

Birthday Party Organizing

Pay Washer and Dryer at Laundromat

Memorial Service

Free Carnation to Cemetery Visitors

Easter Basket Giveaway

Pizza on Moving Day at Apartment or Condo

Lawn Mower Tune-up Clinic

Time Change Reminder Flyer

The Options Are Limitless . . . Use Your Imagination!
Business cards with at least your church or organization's name, address and phone number are highly recommended at all service projects so that people will be able to contact you if they need you in the future. A sample of what we use is listed below:

PROJECT	CONCEPT	EQUIPMENT	PEOPLE NEEDED	COST	WEATHER
Single Mom's Free Oil Change	Most single moms have car problems regularly	Cards,* filters, oil	5 or more	About $6 to $15 per car. Need to give advance notice.	Any weather except extreme cold
Neighborhood Windshield Washing	Going door to door washing windshields in driveways	Cards, squeegees, squirt bottles, cleaner, shop rags	2 or more	Minimal	Cool to warm, but not hot
Mother's Day Carnation Giveaway	Set up outside grocery store on Saturday before Mother's Day	Cards, table, "Free Carnations" sign, cards explaining Mother's Day outreach	5 or more	If you order carnations in advance, you will save significantly	Not a factor
Sunday Morning Paper and Coffee Giveaway	Going door to door early in the morning to houses without a paper in the driveway	Cards, Sunday papers, coffee, cups	2 or more	Papers in bulk cost about $1 each	Any weather but rain
Snow Removal from Driveways and Sidewalks	Help people dig out of the snow	Cards, shovels, coffee, cups	4 or more	Minimal	Snow

PROJECT	CONCEPT	EQUIPMENT	PEOPLE NEEDED	COST	WEATHER
Pulling out Cars Stuck in the Snow	Rescue people from ditches	Cards	2 or more	None	Snow
Empty Garbage Can from Street	Bring cans back to people's houses or garages	Cards	2 or more	None	Any weather
Kitchen Cleanup	Humbling but powerful service	Cards, basic cleaning equipment	2 or more	Minimal	Any weather
Food Delivery to Shut-Ins	Delivering food	Cards	2 or more	None	Any weather
Car Drying at Self-Serve Car Washes	Help dry off cars after they have been washed	Cards, towels or a couple of good chamois	2 or more	Minimal	Car-washing weather
Leaf Raking	Who likes to rake leaves? We do it for them.	Cards, rakes, bags. Blowers work well but are more expensive.	As few as 2—the more the merrier and easier. 10 people can rake a lawn in minutes.	Minimal—you can own your own rake for $5	About any type, but it's tough raking leaves in wet weather

PROJECT	CONCEPT	EQUIPMENT	PEOPLE NEEDED	COST	WEATHER
Christmas Gift Wrap	Everyone needs his or her Christmas gift wrapped. Do it at the mall for free!	Cards, wrapping paper, tape, scissors. Build simple kiosk or booth.	Lots of people needed. Depending on mall traffic, you will need a variety. Use 3 to 10 people per shift.	It can cost as little as $.10 per gift with the right suppliers	If wrapping at an inside location, weather not a problem
Lawn Care	Find unkempt lawns and go for it	Cards; can do basic mowing or more, depending on your desire (edging, trimming, etc.)	2 or more	Cost of gasoline, oil and bags	It's easier to mow dry grass than wet grass
Coke Giveaway	On a hot day, nothing refreshes like a cold drink in Jesus' name	Cards, drinks, ice, clean plastic trash cans for storing cans on ice, table	Minimum of 10	Can lower cost to about $.10 per unit buying in bulk. We gave out 400+ drinks. Ice varies.	Warm or hot weather
Free Coffee	Set up tables at store exits or sporting events and serve hot coffee on cold days	Cards, table, 2 or 3 Igloos® (5 gal.) of coffee, creamers, sugar, stirrers, cups, sign that says "Free Coffee"	3 or more	Minimal	Cool or cold weather

PROJECT	CONCEPT	EQUIPMENT	PEOPLE NEEDED	COST	WEATHER
Popsicle Giveaway	Set up tables at store exits or sporting events and serve Popsicles on warm days	Cards, table, 2 to 3 Igloos®, ice, sign, Popsicles	3 or more	Minimal	Warm weather
Windshield Washing	Hit every car in the lot at stores and shopping centers	Squeegees, squirt bottles with window cleaner, red shop rags, cards**	1 or more—it's more fun with more people.	Minimal	Does not work well in weather over 75 degrees—the liquid evaporates too quickly
Grocery Store Bag Packing	Go to a self-bagging grocery store and help people bag their groceries	Cards, might wear matching aprons, button that says "Just Because"	2 or more	No cost	Good inclement-weather project
Pictionary® in the Park	Start playing Pictionary and strangers just show up	Cards, whiteboard and markers, Pictionary cards	5 or more	Minimal	Warm weather—spring or summer
Balloon Giveaway	Go to a park and give balloons and cards to children with parents	Cards, helium tanks, balloons	2 or more	Balloons and helium are about $.10 to $.15 per child	Any weather when people are at the park

PROJECT	CONCEPT	EQUIPMENT	PEOPLE NEEDED	COST	WEATHER
Free Bird Feeders to Convalescent Hospitals	Share God's love with shut-ins	Cards, bird feeders, birdseed	2 or more	Birdseed, initial investment in feeders	Any weather—greatest appeal in winter
Free House-Number Painting on Curbs	Address numbers painted on the curb	Cards, stencils, spray paint	2 or more	$1 to $2 per house	Dry and warm
Free Community Diner	Throw a party for the neighborhood	Cards, food	15 or more	Depending on meal choice, $2 to $5 per person	Any weather
Coffee Giveaway at a Major Bus Stop	On cold days, people enjoy hot coffee	Cards, coffee, cups, 2 Igloos®, condiments	5 or more	Minimal	Cool or cold weather
Shopping Assistance for Shut-Ins	Shop for those who can't get out on their own	Cards, vehicles	2 or more	Minimal	Any weather
Collect Trees after Christmas	Meet a practical cleanup need	Cards, vehicles	2 or more	None	Any weather
Doggie Dirt Cleanup of Neighborhood Yards	Clean up doggie mess	Cards, pooper scooper (or use plastic bags over hands), bags	2 or more	Minimal	Any weather; very cold is easiest

PROJECT	CONCEPT	EQUIPMENT	PEOPLE NEEDED	COST	WEATHER
Shoe Shining Service	Free shoe shining at stores, malls and other public places	Cards, shoe polish, rags (kits are great)	2 or more	Initial investment minimal	Not a factor if done indoors
Feeding Parking Meters	Find expired parking meters before cars are ticketed and leave a note of explanation	Cards, lots of change	2 or more	You can feed a lot of parking meters for $20	Not a factor except for extreme conditions
Light Bulb Service	Go door to door with light bulbs offering to change burned-out bulbs	Supply of 60-watt light bulbs, cards, step ladder	Teams of 2	Light bulbs are 30 to 50 cents apiece	Not a factor
Laundromat Outreach	Pay for washing machines and dryers at local Laundromats	Cards, rolls of dimes or quarters	Teams of 2—women do best at this—intimidating to have more than a few people	At least $1.50 per wash, $1.00 per dryer	Not a factor
Blood Pressure Screening	Check people's blood pressure at public places	Cards, stethoscopes, sphygmomanometers	Teams of 2 to 4 work well	Initial investment necessary; many nurses have own equipment	Not a factor

PROJECT	CONCEPT	EQUIPMENT	PEOPLE NEEDED	COST	WEATHER
Car Safety Light Check	Replace burned-out bulbs in cars	Cards, variety of spare bulbs to replace burn-outs, screwdrivers	Teams of 2 to 4	Replacement bulbs vary in price	Dry weather works best
Killing Weeds	Spray for weeds and poison ivy on sidewalks and driveways	Cards, weed killer, sprayers, gloves, masks	Teams of 2 to 4	Weed killer varies; least expensive in gallons and diluted into sprayers	Warm, dry; ideally in summer
Seal Blacktop Driveways	Help homeowners seal driveways—best to use flyers to stimulate interest	Cards, sealer, sealer brooms	Teams of 4 to 6	Cost varies	Any weather
House-Gutter Cleaning	Clean gutters on houses to remove leaves, sticks and debris	Cards, gloves, ladders, trash bags	Teams of 2 to 4—everyone needs a ladder.	Plastic bags ongoing purchase after ladders are bought	Dry weather works best
Birthday Party Organizing	Organize and run parties for children—advertise in local papers	Cards, music for party	2 to 4 clowns	Parents pay for supplies; ads placed in free and local papers are best	Any weather

PROJECT	CONCEPT	EQUIPMENT	PEOPLE NEEDED	COST	WEATHER
Door-to-Door Food Collection for the Poor	Put out flyers door to door and then return a week later to pick up cans and dry goods and deliver to poor	Cards, bags given out	Teams of 2	Purchase bags	Not a factor
Car Interior Vacuuming	Set up in mall parking lot or at gas station, and vacuum cars	Cards, several canister vacuums, several hand-held vacuums	Teams of 4 or more	Nothing to purchase if using home vacuum cleaners	Dry weather works best
Filling Windshield Washing Fluid in Cars	Refill washer reserves in cars and clean off wiper blades	Cards, washer fluid, signs, table	Teams of 4 to 10	Fluid commonly costs about $1.00 per gallon	Any weather
Cleaning Fireplaces	Remove ashes from fireplaces	Cards, small brooms, small flat shovels	Teams of 2	Purchase trash bags; possible initial investment on tools	Usually a cool-weather project
Checking Air on Tires	See if tires are properly inflated—adjust pressure if necessary	Cards, compressor or portable air "bubbles," air pressure gauges	Teams of 4 to 6	Pressure gauges not much; borrow compressors or air tanks	Almost any weather; but people are more concerned in summer

PROJECT	CONCEPT	EQUIPMENT	PEOPLE NEEDED	COST	WEATHER
Memorial Service	Advertise complimentary memorial service in newspaper or telephone books	Cards	Pastor and others to set up and take down	Advertising	Not a factor
Radon Detectors	Give out complimentary detectors in areas where radon is a concern. Return in a few days.	Cards, detectors	Teams of 2	In quantity, these cost about $10 each	Not a factor
Carbon Monoxide Detectors	Give out complimentary carbon monoxide detectors. Come back in a few days to check.	Cards, detectors	Teams of 2	In quantity, these cost about $3.50 each	Usually a winter project
Smoke Detector Batteries	Give out complimentary smoke detector batteries for refills	Cards, reminders with date, batteries	Teams of 2	In quantity, these cost about $1.25 per battery	Any weather
Toilet Cleaning	Clean toilets of restaurants and stores	Cards, urinal screens, cleaning supplies	Teams of 2	Supply costs vary, but minimal	Any weather

PROJECT	CONCEPT	EQUIPMENT	PEOPLE NEEDED	COST	WEATHER
Outdoor Window Washing	Wash first-floor windows	Cards, professional squeegees and cleaner, short ladder, buckets	2 or more	One-time purchase of squeegees (not too expensive)	50 degrees or warmer
Yard Cleanup	Look for messy yards	Cards, trash bags, rakes	2 or more	Minimal	Any weather
Easter Basket Giveaway	Every child wants an Easter basket	Cards, baskets. We put in candy, Christian literature, and once even Christian tapes	2 or more	Costs vary from $3 to $5 per basket	Not a factor
Rainy Day Grocery Escort	Help shoppers with packages to their car	Cards, golf umbrellas	2 or more	Minimal	Rainy days
Windshield Washing at Self-Serve Gas Station	Revive the practice of free windshield washing with fill-up	Cards, squeegees, squirt bottles, red rags, cleaner	2 or more	Initial purchase of equipment (minimal)	Works best in clear weather. If it's too hot, the cleaner will evaporate.

PROJECT	CONCEPT	EQUIPMENT	PEOPLE NEEDED	COST	WEATHER
House/Apartment Repair	Fix broken things. Limit repairs to your capabilities.	Cards, basic tool kit	2 or more capable repair people. Don't send unskilled workers—they can make things worse.	Limit your work to your budget. We did a lot of winterizing at a low cost.	Not a factor
House/Apartment /Dorm Cleaning	Who doesn't need housework help?	Cards, vacuum cleaners, brooms, trash bags	2 or more	Minimal	Any weather—may need to call ahead or work from referrals
Winter Car Wash	Spray off salt and road grime	Cards, coffee supplies, wands to spray off underside of cars	10 or more	Minimal	Don't attempt this in weather below 20 degrees—could freeze door locks
Summer Car Wash	Free car wash! We used banners that said "Free Car Wash— No Kidding"	Cards, basic wash equipment, banners. Can also serve drinks, play music and provide lawn chairs.	Minimum of 12, but 25 to 30 preferred. We did 2 to 3 cars at once. Designate an "evangelist" to talk to people.	Minimal. We often used a sports bar's parking lot and paid for the water.	Above 60 degrees. Overcast days don't work well. People won't stop if it looks like it may rain.

* Cards should have your fellowship name, phone, meeting time(s) and easy-to-follow map on back.

** This card reads: "While you were away from your car, people from the Vineyard Christian Fellowship washed your windshield."

MORE KINDNESS

If you are a fan of the film *Ferris Bueller's Day Off,* I'm sure you've seen the famous scene at the end of the credits. As the credits come to a close, Ferris comes out with a towel wrapped around his head and says, "You still here? Why are you still here? Leave! It's time to leave! Now get out of here! Enough already! Leave!"

It occurs to me that little clip might well be shown to all alive churches each and every week, 52 weeks a year! We need to be reminded of our reason for being. "Enough already! Go and do the works of Jesus, every day and in every way!"

Here are five more simple projects that can be used by ordinary people to show kindness every day . . .

1. *Go to the same watering hole every day and spread God's love by being generous to the next customer in line.* Develop regular places where you go for coffee, orange juice or a burrito as big as your head! As you near the front of the line and begin to engage the cashier, turn to the next person in line and say: "What are you having? This one's on me." Be prepared, with a big smile on your face, to answer protests and questions with inspired responses. One response: "I know you can pay for your own, but I just wanted to show you God's love in a practical way." Hand them a connect card from your church or from kindness.com, and be open to any way you might answer a question or meet their need.

2. *Pass along a little sweetness.* This kindness touch involves Tic-Tacs, Hershey Kisses or chewing gum. As you meet receptionists, customer service people or others in the waiting room at the doctor's office, hand them

a prepared baggie containing some goodies with a kindness.com card attached and say, "You look like you could use a spoonful of kindness today, and God sent me here to give you one!"

3. *Give a little recognition.* A friend of mine was flying recently and had a persistent cough. The flight attendant was particularly attentive to keeping his water cup full. He took out a kindness.com card and wrote a little note: "Thanks for being so kind to me today. You really did a great job!" and signed his name.

4. *Leave a generous tip.* Recognize when a waitperson provides extra special service and leave a kindness.com card attached to your minimum 30-percent tip. Write a personal note saying "Thanks for doing such a great job serving me." On the way out, seek out the manager and tell him or her what a great job your waitperson did.

5. *Top off the tank.* Be alert when you are filling up your car with gasoline (most of us are doing more and more of that these days, more and more often!). Pay attention, someone nearby could use some extra gas. Offer to add $5 or $10 to the tank, and simply hand the person the cash with a kindness.com card. This is guaranteed to bring a response! Be ready to follow God's lead.

Evangelism Assumptions

by Doug Murren, Doug Roe
and Steve Sjogren

Let these statements help you step out with confidence into service evangelism.

1. Deep down non-Christians really want to know and obey God.
2. Non-Christians typically have five or more significant encounters with the gospel before coming into a relationship with Jesus Christ.
3. Non-Christians usually won't come to us to find God. We have to go to them.
4. Evangelism is the easiest and most natural of all the ministries in the church.
5. Effective evangelism requires little training.
6. Friendly, openhearted people make the best evangelists.
7. Church life, spent in the presence of Christians only, produces saints who are neither friendly nor openhearted to outsiders.
8. The kingdom of God is the primary mission and issue of our shared life as Christians, not self-preservation or the perpetuation of a church.

9. The primary foundation of all our evangelism is love.

10. Placing expectations upon someone we're evangel-
    izing is always injurious and works against that per-
    son coming to Christ.

11. We become holy and righteous by identifying with
    Jesus and surrendering to His will for us rather than
    trying to obey the law.

12. Each person in relationship with Jesus is primarily
    responsible for his or her own follow-up and fellow-
    ship needs.

13. The Holy Spirit is the only true evangelist who has
    ever existed, as well as the only disciple-maker.

14. It is normal for everyone who loves Jesus to have a
    heart for the poor, sick, lost, widowed and homeless.

15. We are committed to prayer as an essential element
    of any successful outreach venture. Because we
    highly value active obedience to the will of God, an
    ideal time to pray is on the way to share God's love
    with others.

16. Non-Christians may not remember what they've been
    told regarding God's love, but they always remember
    what they've experienced of God's love.

17. None of us can manufacture the genuine working
    of the Holy Spirit.

18. The Holy Spirit is able, willing and free to break
    in and carry on His work in unspectacular, non-
    manipulative and surprising ways.

19. An atmosphere of anointing, freshness and vitality
    comes upon believers when they spend time with
    non-Christians.

20. Because of irrational fears, the average evangelical
    Christian today has no plans to participate actively
    in evangelism.

21. Most Christians are so far out of touch with the world around them that they know little of its fears, problems, concerns or issues.

22. Because God is highly committed to the lost, almost any evangelistic approach will work given enough time and commitment to sharing the good news.

23. God has a passionate heart for the lost. Whether we choose to bring Christ to unbelievers or not, God is very creative and will always seek to win them in some way.

24. It is a privilege to be involved in the process of sharing God's love with those He is inviting into the family of God.

25. Effective evangelism is more of a mindset and paradigm than a program.

26. Our evangelism is really an overflow of our relationship with God and our relationships with people.

27. In order to effectively evangelize our cities, we will need to make major time commitments to sharing our lives with the lost. In fact, God may ask us to dedicate the rest of our lives to the task of reaching our cities with the gospel.

28. The value of evangelism will regularly conflict with day-to-day programs of church life.

29. Because they are central to the mission of the local church, funding for evangelism and ministry to the poor ought to be seen as a part of the regular church budget rather than areas to be financed by special offerings.

Recommended Reading

Aldrich, Joe. *Gentle Persuasion*. Portland, OR: Multnomah, 1988. Aldrich speaks from his many years of experience as a friendship evangelist. He has done an outstanding job of maintaining relationships with not-yet Christians while working in the ministry—something not many pastors manage to do. His enthusiasm is contagious.

Cook, Jerry, with Stanley C. Baldwin. *Love, Acceptance and Forgiveness*. Ventura, CA: Regal, 1979. I consider this a modern-day classic work on the application of God's grace to the daily Christian life. The principles Cook presents will cause you to examine your own church's way of approaching outsiders.

Dennison, Jack. *City Reaching*. Pasadena, CA: William Carey Publishing, 1999. This is one of the most exciting books that I've read in the past several years. Dennison presents a bold and hopeful view for the Church's future, but not one that will be free from radically different ways of doing things. I especially resonated with his vision for church planting.

Erwin, Gayle D. *The Jesus Style*. Waco, TX: Word, 1983. Erwin convincingly presents the life of Jesus as one of supreme servanthood. This book will make you uncomfortable unless you are willing to take one giant step forward in serving others. I would put it at the top of my list of books related to servant evangelism.

Gerber, Michael. *The E Myth*. New York: Ballinger-Harper & Row, 1986. Anyone involved in a growing ministry that is innovative will find this a very helpful treatment on the misunderstandings common among entrepreneurs.

Kawasaki, Guy. *Selling the Dream*. New York: Harper Collins, 1991. As a former "software evangelist" for Apple computers, Kawasaki explored the implications of selling a new idea. Many of his ideas carry over to Christian evangelism. Part of his discovery process included attending the Billy Graham School of Evangelism.

Ladd, George E. *The Gospel of the Kingdom*. Grand Rapids, MI: Eerdmans, 1959. Ladd's insights into the presences of the kingdom of God have had an enormous impact on evangelicals over the past 30 years, and have specifically influenced the development of my thinking as I developed servant evangelism.

Lewis, Robert. *The Church of Irresistible Influence*. Grand Rapids, MI: Zondervan, 2001. Lewis and his church in Little Rock have taken the basic idea of servant evangelism and run with it. They have taken on large projects on a city-wide level, such as rehabbing schools. After doing these projects for years now, they have seen amazing results and have developed great influence in the community and state.

Little, Paul. *How to Give Away Your Faith*. Downers Grove, IL: InterVarsity Press, 1966. Little's book has helped many fearful Christians step into the arena of evangelism over the past several decades. It continues to prove itself a classic.

McLaren, Brian D. *Finding Faith*. Grand Rapids, MI: Zondervan, 2000. There are lots of evidences that our culture is very interested in spiritual things. That perspective is one that sometimes runs counter to the popular opinion of the Church. Written in the tradition of C. S. Lewis in *Mere Christianity* and Scott Peck's *The Road Less Traveled*, this book challenges the reader to think in terms of how one believes more than what one believes. A great book for bridging the gap with not-yet Christians.

McLaren, Brian D. *More Ready Than You Realize*. Grand Rapids, MI: Zondervan, 2002. How open to God are not-yet believers to begin to follow God in a personal way? McLaren argues that they are more open than most Christians tend to think. We have simply tended to put seekers into categories that fit our mental frameworks nicely, but don't do them a lot of good. He compares the approach to coming to Christ to a dance between the church and the unchurched. Reading this will make you eager to go to the dance.

McManus, Erwin R. *An Unstoppable Force: Daring to Become the Church God Had in Mind*. Loveland, CO: Group, 2001. What would happen if God actually got His way with the Church? McManus ponders that question and comes up with some thoughts about the Church that are exciting and challenging. Don't read this one unless you are ready for your view of the Church to be rocked a bit.

Mittelberg, Mark, and Bill Hybels. *Building a Contagious Church*. Grand Rapids, MI: Zondervan, 2000. Here are principles and proven practices from historic Willow Creek Church on how to build a church atmosphere that is truly contagious. Mittelberg speaks from the accrued experience of years of living this stuff out in Chicago.

Ortiz, Juan Carlos. *Disciple*. Lake Mary, FL: Creation House, 1975. This is a refreshing little book that is very helpful to new believers. It has helped many thousands of Christians find their way forward into a simple, childlike Christianity that emphasizes obedience.

Pippert, Rebecca Manley. *Out of the Saltshaker & Into the World*. Downers Grove, IL: InterVarsity Press, 1979. Pippert confesses to being a timid evangelist. Her quotable line is, "Only two groups struggle with evangelism: Christians and non-Christians." She gives encouragement for Christians to form and maintain significant relationships with those not yet in Christ. She offers principles for personal evangelism that are timeless and golden. This book is essential for your library.

Random Acts of Kindness, a compilation. Berkeley, CA: Conari, 1993. Though not a "Christian" book, this compilation of stories gives testimony to the power of kindness in the lives of many. Many ideas are shared for meeting needs in others' lives. Some of them are practical and easily adaptable to servant evangelism.

Roxburgh, Alan J. *The Missionary Congregation, Leadership and Liminality*. Harrisburg, PA: Trinity Press International, 1997. In this small book, Roxburgh explains that the modern church has been pushed into a chaplain's role in society. He offers no easy answers to the matters we face, but concludes that we must become missionary congregations

emerging into the world. A very thought-provoking, helpful book.

Scazzero, Pete. *Introducing Jesus*. Downers Grove, IL: InterVarsity
Press, 1991. The author of many popular study guides,
Scazzero offers us many insights into sharing Christ with
friends and family. He writes with authority and fire as an
effective personal evangelist who has had fruitful ministry
for years.

Sjogren, Steve. *101 Ways to Reach Your Community*. Colorado
Springs, CO: NavPress, 2001. This is a follow-up to *Conspiracy
of Kindness*. It is a virtual cookbook of outreach projects that
are laid out in simple, moderate, and more complex projects.
All that is needed for each project is clearly spelled out. This
is a great resource for small groups who have gotten the basic
idea of servant evangelism down and are ready to go for it.

Sjogren, Steve and Janie. *101 Ways to Reach Those in Need*.
Colorado Springs, CO: NavPress, 2002. Similar to the above
guidebook, this one is directed to those who are interested
in specifically reaching out to the needy. It contains a lot of
practical tips on how to begin to minister to the needy and
assumes the reader is starting out with little or no experience. The projects are varied and creative. Both of these
books can be ordered at the servant evangelism website
(www.servantevangelism.com).

Sweet, Leonard. *Aquachurch*. Loveland, CO: Group, 2000. Sweet is
simply the foremost interpreter of our culture in the Church
today. I buy all of his books because his insights on post-
modernity are so sharp. *Aquachurch* argues that the Church
exists in a time and place of flux and we need to be ready to

flow with the changing times around us if we hope to have any impact.

Wimber, John, with Kevin Springer. *Power Evangelism*. Ventura, CA: Regal, 2009. Wimber has helped many Christians see ministry in a new way. *Power Evangelism* will challenge you to examine your own assumptions about evangelism.

ALSO FROM STEVE SJOGREN

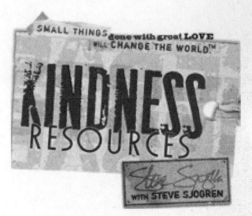

Also Available by Steve Sjogren

An Unforgettable Story of Life After Death

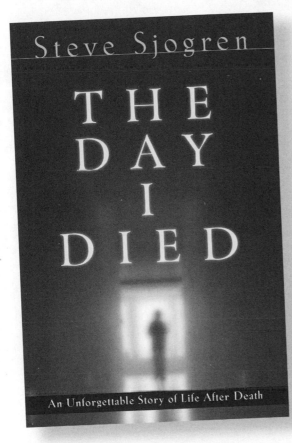

The Day I Died
An Unforgettable Story
of Life After Death
Steve Sjogren
ISBN 978.08307.38120

"The cold voice of the anesthesiologist recited the typical 'Count backward from 10' routine. And darkness closed around me before I got to 7. That's when I found out what it's like to die—and to come back from the dead."

It was a beautiful winter's day, showing no signs of what was to come. Steve Sjogren, pastor of one of America's fastest growing churches, went into the hospital for routine gall bladder surgery and died—twice.

What began as a tragic medical accident led to Steve's encounter with death, an experience of unimaginable peace and some surprises, with comforting words from God, a meeting with an angel, and seeing those who had died before him.

In *The Day I Died*, you will read Steve Sjogren's unforgettable story and catch a glimpse of the hereafter. Discover how he learned a myriad of lessons about hearing God's voice in times of crisis, how he came to trust God in a new way during the recovery process and how his life has changed as a result of this experience.

If you, or someone you know, are fearful of dying, curious about heaven or simply desiring to live life to its fullest, this encouraging book could change how you view life and death.